TALES OF THE LOCH

Tales of the Loch

BRUCE SANDISON

MAINSTREAM
PUBLISHING

FOR ANN
my fishing friend

Grateful thanks to the following publishers for their kind permissions: Aberdeen University Press (*Midges in Scotland* by George Hendry), Constable and Co (*The Scottish Peaks* by W. A. Poucher), Peter Davies (*Fishing from Afar* by Stephen Johnson) and to Michael J. Robson for the extract from *Tibbie Shiels*.

First published in Great Britain 1990 by
MAINSTREAM PUBLISHING COMPANY (EDINBURGH) LTD
7 Albany Street
Edinburgh EH1 3UG

ISBN 1 85158 350 5 (cloth)

British Library Cataloguing in Publication Data
Sandison, Bruce
  Tales of the Loch
  1. Scotland. Angling.
  I. Title
  920.0411

ISBN 1-85158-350-5

Typeset in Great Britain by Beecee Typesetting Services
Printed in Great Britain by Mackays of Chatham Plc, Kent

CONTENTS

INTRODUCTION

*ALES OF THE LOCH* collects together events and memories of nearly forty years' game fishing. These stories first appeared on BBC Radio Scotland and were subsequently re-broadcast on Radio 4. The series has run for five years, due largely to the patience and endurance of Chris Lowell, the BBC Senior Producer with whom I worked. Because of the limitations of programme time, material I would have liked to have used had to be excluded.

This book has given me the opportunity of rectifying that matter; and also the opportunity of thanking Chris Lowell for his support during the making of the radio programmes. It was never easy. No matter how well prepared we thought we were, we always seemed to end up the night before, poring over details into the small hours; books, maps and papers scattered everywhere. Chris is a perfectionist. Everything had to be right. Every time.

All the programmes were recorded outside, sometimes in the snow, often in pouring rain. Local people became accustomed to seeing two heads, above a sheltering bale of hay in the middle of a field, talking animatedly to a sock — to shield the microphone from wind.

My experience of broadcasting prior to recording the series was zero; but Chris is a marvellous tutor; knowing exactly when to smile encouragingly, and exactly when to curse roundly. However, the result of our efforts seemed to give pleasure to a lot of people, and I am delighted to be able to bring the stories together in book form.

I would also like to thank my publisher, Bill Campbell, for giving me the opportunity of doing so. Bill patiently suffered my excuses and delays in delivering the text, and, as always, has always been the perfect publisher: supportive, considerate and courteous.

Most of all, I offer grateful thanks to my wife, Ann, who, as always, has guided me through the toils and tribulations of writing this book. Without her encouragement it would never have seen the light of morning, let alone day.

Bruce Sandison
Ruther House
Watten
Caithness

STRATHBEG

TRATHBEG is a naturalist's paradise and a trout fisherman's delight. Stocked with a Loch Leven strain of brown trout, this excellent game fishery lies at the heart of one of Scotland's most important nature reserves. Home and haven to thousands of wildfowl. More than 24,000 birds have been counted at Strathbeg during the course of a single day, and many more visit the reserve throughout the year.

Most spectacular are huge flocks of Scandinavian greylag and pink-footed geese, which winter-roost at Strathbeg, grazing in surrounding fields; as well as smaller numbers of less common barnacle geese, resting on their tiring journey from Spitzbergen in Norway to Solway Firth feeding grounds.

Hundreds of graceful Icelandic whooper swans arrive in October and November. Their haunting call echoes across the loch on cold, still winter nights. From September, smaller ducks fly in: tufted, pochard, goldeneye, mallard, wigeon, mergansers, goosander and smew. Mute swan, stately and serene, are present all the year. The last time I visited Strathbeg, I counted eighty elegant swans, floating galleon-like on calm waters.

One hundred and eighty-six different species of birds have been noted at Strathbeg, including rarities such as Caspian tern, little egret, crane, pied-billed grebe and red-footed falcon; amongst nesting residents are shelduck, mallard, tufted duck, secretive water rail, sedge and willow warbler, black-bibbed reed bunting and diminutive wren.

Strathbeg lies on the north-east coast of Scotland, between the once flourishing fishing ports of Peterhead and Fraserburgh, close to the village of Crimond. The reserve is part owned and part leased by the Royal Society for the Protection of Birds, ably managed by RSPB resident warden, Jimmy Dunbar.

The loch covers an area of 550 acres, surrounded north, west and south by farm lands and fresh-water marshes. To the east, the loch is separated from the North Sea by the Black Bar. These deserted sand dunes host an amazing variety of wild flowers: heath and marsh bedstraw, ragwort, meadow vetchling, tufted vetch, marsh cinquefoil, felwort, angelica, marsh valerian, and that Buchan beauty, grass of Parnassus; as well as rare orchids: spotted, and butterfly orchid.

You may also see otters, or their pug marks, where they slip quietly into the loch, keeping Strathbeg trout alert and fit. Badger, roe deer, weasel and stoat live by the shore, as do field vole and shrew; ideal prey for hunting raptors: sparrowhawk, short-eared owl and that most lovely of all falcons, diminutive merlin.

Strathbeg is connected to the sea by Rattray Burn, and before 1700 the loch was part of a tidal estuary, well used by Roman, then Viking warships seeking refuge from storms. In the sixteenth century, Mary, Queen of Scots, conferred the honour of Royal Burgh on the community that grew up around the estuary.

Decades of silt, washed downstream by winter floods, blocked the bay; and a great sand storm in the early eighteenth century closed the harbour; but, at the same time, happily for thousands of birds and generations of anglers, the loch was formed: the largest dune-slack lake in Britain.

Strathbeg is bordered on its landward side by a vast, derelict, World War II airfield; deserted, pock-marked runways lead to the base of a Ministry of Defence 900-foot-high radio mast, surrounded by ancillary buildings. Although these structures dominate the scene, once you are afloat, fishing, or camera-stalking wildfowl, they never impinge upon the mind's eye.

South end Strathbeg is the principal mooring bay; close to the seventeenth-century home of the Lairds of Haddo, now a farmhouse. Eastwards are the ruins of the ancient Chapel of St Mary, reputed to have been founded in 911 AD; bounded by the marram grass-covered sand dunes of Rattray Head.

Strathbeg is one of the least known and yet most delightful lochs in Scotland and I was aware of its reputation, having discovered it whilst researching my book *The Trout Lochs of Scotland*, although I had never fished there.

When my oldest son Blair said farewell sadly to the Outer Hebrides and came to work in Aberdeenshire, my wife Ann and I arranged to spend a few days there, fishing and exploring a country that neither of us knew. Our first port of call was Strathbeg; and as we drove through Crimond on our way to the loch, I smiled at the inscription on the face of the church clock: "The Hour is Coming". At last. I was to see Loch of Strathbeg.

See was the operative word. Our party included Blair, his wife Barbara, Ann and myself. The boat held three. We parked near the boathouse on the west shore, a ruined, mud-filled RAF building, where I pushed and heaved my three companions afloat, waving a cheerful farewell. Wishing them "Tight Lines". Whilst they fished I explored the shores, haunting the hides, marvelling at the variety of bird, plant and animal life. The day flew by so quickly that I hardly noticed evening stealing in on crimson wings.

The anglers returned triumphant, with a beautiful, silver basket of six fine trout. I was as pleased with the sights and sounds of my day — treasured memories.

Bank fishing is *verboten* on Strathbeg because of the importance to nesting birds of surrounding marsh-lands, privacy being essential when engaged in the serious business of propitiating species. Fishing is from boats only, but outboard motors are allowed. Welcome relief on this exposed, often windy water.

Strathbeg fishes best in a decent wind, and trout average 12oz in weight, although one was caught recently that tipped the scales at over 3lb. However, size is never important to "proper" anglers. Strathbeg trout reward effort by their fighting spirit; and these lovely fish are great characters, regardless of size.

Strathbeg trout are not the only characters in Buchan. That area of Aberdeenshire has a long tradition of producing outstanding personalities. George Halket (1690-1756), schoolmaster in the parish of Rathen, songwriter, satirist and Hanoverian scourge. Halket, a staunch Jacobite, is remembered for his satirical lyric: "Whirry, Whigs, awa', Man", and for his fine song "Logie O' Buchan". The location of the events described in Logie is Crimond, by Strathbeg, where the principal character,

James Robertson, was the laird's gardener. Another Halket satire: "A dialogue between the Devil and George II", an imaginary, scurrilous discussion which did nothing for King George's reputation, so incensed his son, Butcher Cumberland, that he offered £100 reward to anyone who would bring him Halket's body. Dead or alive. Needless to say the reward remained uncollected. Buchan people take care of their own.

Halket's famous contemporary, Lord Pitsligo, who commanded a regiment at the Battle of Culloden, also benefited from deeply ingrained Buchan loyalties. After the disaster, Pitsligo spent many years in hiding, close to his old Buchan home. Although local people must have known his hiding place, he was never betrayed. Pitsligo died there in 1767, head, much to his surprise, still firmly attached to his unrepentant shoulders.

Blair's Aberdeenshire home was a less perilous residence, a delightful cottage at Shivas, set amidst mature woodlands, loud with bird song and surrounded by rich, fertile fields. House of Shivas, nearby, was built in the sixteenth century, destroyed by fire in 1900 and has now been restored. James III's astrologer and physician, Archbishop William Scheves of St Andrews, is a descendant from the old family.

Scheves was not a popular choice for the pre-eminent religious position in Scotland, but he was a "King's man" and was consecrated in Holyrood in 1479, in spite of "the double handicap of illegitimacy and non-baronial parentage". Scheves acquitted himself well, and is described by Leslie J. Macfarlane in the *Innes Review* as "a cultured and learned man with a genuine love of his country and its history, a conscientious archbishop who late in life turned to theology, a generous benefactor to the University of St Andrews".

We had also determined to acquit ourselves well in the removal of fish from their natural habitat, and Blair and I set out one evening intent upon playing havoc with Ythan sea-trout. The night was mild and windless. Sea-trout jumped and splashed enticingly. All refused to bite. Unlike Ythan midges. After three hours' fruitless effort, we were driven from the river by their incessant attack. I have suffered the ungentle ministrations of midges throughout Scotland, from Cape Wrath to Loch Lomond-side, but few match the ferocity of Ythan's ladies. It took three pints of home brew, each, before we stopped scratching.

Aberdeenshire is best known as the place to go for salmon fishing, and the Royal Dee is one of the finest salmon streams in Scotland. It is where Arthur Wood gained fishing immortality by devising the greased line method of catching salmon in low water conditions, using a small fly called a Blue Charm. Or so it is reported. When I was researching my book, *The Sporting Gentleman's Gentleman*, stories from Scottish keepers, stalkers and gillies, Jimmy Ross of Rothes told me a different tale about Arthur Wood and his "wee Blue Charm". Jimmy was talking to Wood's gillie one night, asking him about his gentleman's astonishing success with the small fly: "Wee Blue Charm be damned. It's a great Jock Scott that's doing all the damage," came the reply.

The Don, Dee's near neighbour can also produce superb sport with salmon; but less well known is the fact that the Don is perhaps the finest trout stream in the world. To give an example, a 7lb trout was caught recently; a huge fish for any loch, let alone river. Fish of over 3lb are frequently taken, mostly by dry fly experts fishing the evening rise. Anglers study the river, locating where the big fish lie, and creep up at dusk when fish are least likely to suspect foul play. As a party of French anglers did, whilst staying at the Grant Arms, Monymusk, in May 1987 for three days. During their visit they caught 115 trout of between 1lb and 4lb in weight. I am pleased to report all but specimen fish, trout of over 3lb, were returned to fight another day. My regard for things Gaelic shot up when I heard that story. I concluded that there might be some good after all in the Common Market.

Monymusk is the fishing centre for the Don. The Grant Arms Hotel, run by Colin Hart, offers excellent salmon and trout fishing opportunities, comfortable accommodation and first-class advice on the fly of the moment; and which fingers to cross.

I am careful about fingers when fishing the Don, particularly Ann's. We once spent an afternoon on our favourite Don beat, between Slatestone and Holly Bush Pot, by splendid Paradise Wood. This most perfect of all forests was laid out by Lord Cullen in 1719 and is dappled with an amazing variety of trees: oak, ash, elm, copper beech, larch, spruce and magnificent, statuesque Scots pine.

At the end of the day, being a gentleman, I offered to carry Ann's rod back to the car; but she is a very independent lady and announced that she was perfectly capable of carrying her own fishing-rod. In the ensuing tussle, the middle fly on her cast, a size 14 Grouse & Claret, sank into the tip of the third finger of her left hand.

Ann disappeared behind a tree: "Do you want any help?" I offered, sheepishly. "No," came the stern reply. A few moments later, somewhat red-faced, Ann appeared, the fly having been removed. "Give me my rod, please," was all she said.

Unlike the Dee, which is essentially a Highland spate stream, rushing urgently from Grampian heights to its meeting with the North Sea, Don pursues a more leisurely course; meandering through the countryside, lingering in wide, deep pools, sliding gracefully beneath branches of ancient trees. Don is a lady. Dee, a brash, bustling girl.

Aberdeenshire farmers, who know a thing or six about land, will tell you that "a mile o' Dons worth twa o' Dee" and whilst the Dee is crystal clear, Don tends to be more coloured and weedy. I know, from deep, personal experience. Six feet deep.

Ann and I were fishing Forbes Castle Water. I was inching carefully down the south bank of Dam Pool, covering every possible lie, when a good trout rose behind me. I walked back to have a cast at him. A fool's errand. You never catch these brutes. Having rejected your fly once, they are hardly likely to have changed their minds in the space of a couple of minutes.

But in spite of nearly forty years' experience, I can never resist temptation. Tall reeds fringed the bank. Cut, but not removed, they had fallen forward, still "hinged", so to speak, to the bank, giving the impression of terra firma. I was perfectly well aware of this fact. Water, not solid ground, lay beneath.

I cast into the pool, in the general direction of where the trout had risen. To my astonishment, I saw a huge trout, at least 7lb in weight, rushing from the cover of a rock ledge towards my fly. I froze, mouth trout-like, agape in anticipation, heart racing. I saw the glass case over the mantle, filled. Fortune and fame at last.

The trout grabbed. It happened in a flash, although in retrospect everything seemed to occur in slow motion, as though I were watching from another planet. The strength of the great trout was such that, when it turned and ran, I stepped forward, involuntarily. On to the treacherous reeds. I did a neat somersault and found myself on the bottom of the river, drowning; fishing jacket, waders and fishing bag weighed me down. I opened my eyes. Swaying gently in the current were weeds. Beautiful, green fronds. Mesmerising. This is it, I thought. Here I go.

Scenes from my childhood flashed before my eyes. Then I remembered the £500-worth of photographic gear in my fishing bag, and the thought of damaging that galvanised me into action. I managed, with difficulty, to struggle upright, my nose just clearing the surface. I still had the rod, gripped vice-like; and, miraculously, the trout was still on, reel still screaming in anger. What to do? Save my cameras or fight the fish. Cameras won, and in chucking my fishing bag ashore, the 4lb breaking-strain cast snapped and the trout was gone.

I waded to the bank, shoulder deep, and struggled ashore. Dripping, shaking, absolutely stunned. I cursed my ill-fortune and stupidity. Anglers wait a lifetime for such a chance, and I had botched mine.

The sun was shining hotly, so I stripped off and spread my garments out to dry, contemplating my wrack. At least the cameras had survived. Everything else was wet through. A voice from the far bank roused me. Ann's. "All right, dear? Having fun?" I had nearly drowned, just lost the largest trout I was ever likely to see, and she asks if I am having fun? "You don't happen to have a cigarette and some dry matches, Ann, do you?" I replied.

When I explained, I got even less sympathy: "Of all the stupid things. Call yourself experienced." At lunch it was worse. "How big was the trout, Dad? Pulled you right into the river, did it? There, there, what a fright that must have been. What did you say you had in your hip flask?" I made a mental note to seek revenge at the earliest opportunity.

The Don has always been kind to me and my opportunity for revenge came sooner, rather than later. Blair's job took him to troutless Humberside, but after two years, good fortune posted him back to Aberdeenshire.

In September 1989, that most disastrous of all salmon fishing seasons, Blair and I were downstream from Paradise Wood. Don was low, little more than bare bones, and there was no point in fishing for salmon; so we had decided to trout fish.

Towards the end of the beat, the stream is divided by a small island. Blair reached it first and carefully fished the north channel, catching nothing. I watched. He waded ashore and we had a planning conference on the shingle. "I will have a few casts here,

Blair, then follow you down to the next pool," I suggested. "No, Father," came the reply. "That would not be fair. At your age, advancing years and all that. I would like to see you catch one more trout. You fish the next pool first."

Ignoring the veiled insult, I insisted, and Blair set off, leaving me to my own devices. If ever a pool held good fish, I thought, then this is one. The water swirled in over small pebbles, widening into a narrow, deep, fast-flowing stream; shaded from sunlight by overhanging branches.

Halfway down the pool, and quite unexpectedly, a good fish rose and slashed at my cast, taking the tail fly, a size 14 Peter Ross. I couldn't believe my luck. With the reel screaming in protest and the fish performing acrobatics all round the pool I prayed the hook would hold.

It was like reliving the Dam Pool experience all over again, this time from above the water, rather than underneath it. As the trout began to tire, I fumbled for the landing net. No landing net. Blair had it. "Blair!" I called weakly. "Blair!" loudly, in desperation. No answer.

Taking courage in both hands, I began to steer the fish towards the shingle beach. As the water shallowed, the trout, sensing danger, tugged viciously and tore off to sulk in the middle of the pool. I died a thousand deaths before I got him ashore, but eventually, at the fourth attempt, I managed to beach the fish.

Delighted, I laid the trout on the shingle and went in search of Blair. He came wandering towards me, obviously having admitted defeat, and I fell in beside him, companionably in step. As we walked up the river I began a monologue about how difficult it was to catch Don trout.

"Not a river for beginners, Blair," I explained. "You really have to be an expert to have any chance of success. Mere mortals, average, run-of-the-mill duffers don't stand a chance." And much more in a similar vain. Blair, fishless, was happy to agree.

As we reached the island pool, I suggested Blair had a few more casts before finishing. Reluctantly, and without much enthusiasm, Blair clambered down the river bank and waded across the stream. Two seconds later, he spotted the big trout.

"Oh, by the way, Blair," I called, "whilst you are there, would you mind bringing me the fish I caught in the stream? You know, where you were fishing? Can you believe it, I almost forgot that I had left it there?" Revenge is sweet. And catching a 3lb Don trout is even sweeter.

ORKNEY

APS fascinate me. Poring over a world atlas or 1:50,000 sheet gives me as much pleasure as actually visiting the places I dream about. Perhaps even more so, because with maps, my illusions remain intact, unblemished by reality.

From time to time, generally during long, cold winter months, suffering from wander-lust, I descend upon my local library like some latter-day Robinson Crusoe, anxious to return to desert island life. I could never understand why Crusoe left his paradise in the first place; wild horses would not have dragged me from Juan Fernandez.

I armchair travel the globe in front of December's fires, from Greenland's icy mountains, to India's coral strand: exploring the unending vista of Asia's central plains; picking my dangerous way through steaming Amazonian jungles; scaling South America's towering peaks; sailing the seven seas; buffeting round Cape Horn.

It is a harmless pastime, and to supplement reading I send for mounds of travel brochures to help feed my fantasies. Consequently, over the years, I have become knowledgeable about many of the world's remote places. When the time comes, I know exactly where I shall hide: "far from the madding crowd".

Islands particularly hold my interest. Be they shimmering Aegean jewels, or blue, mist-shrouded moments in the Outer Hebrides, they all induce in me an overwhelming urge just to drop everything and be gone. Probably a question of greener grass, but I find the call of the wild irresistible.

When I served Queen and Country, and was Orderly Officer one night, I received a signal marked "TOP SECRET". I hurried to the Adjutant and he opened it to find an urgent request for a volunteer to serve in Southern Arabia. Three days later, I was on my way. But even then, once there, my greatest desire was to escape to Socotra, an island in the Indian Ocean.

My wife Ann is also a dreamer, but far more practical. She pores over time-tables: bus, rail, ship and plane, and travels her secret world in cookery-books. We have one of the most extensive and comprehensive private collections of cook-books in the North; and her library keeps growing.

Most Saturday evenings, during winter, Ann prepares an ethnic meal from the current country of her dreams: Turkey, Mexico, Egypt, Indonesia, Arabia; or historic dishes from England's past, and even delights from Roman times. Splendid, memorable moments.

But over the years, because of the dictates of bank balance and burgeoning family, we have spent much of our time exploring Scotland; and our love of game fishing has provided a marvellous excuse for tramping moor and mountain in seach of peace, seclusion, and a few wild brown trout.

Twelve miles from our Caithness home, across the stormy waters of the Pentland Firth, lie the Orkney Islands, and from the hill behind Ruther House we can see the pinnacle stack of the Old Man of Hoy. On a clear day Hoy, "the high island", seems so near that one imagines one might stretch out a hand and run fingers down its jagged red cliffs.

The wilderness of Hoy belies the fertile, gentle nature of the other Orkney islands. Mainland is famous for the quality of its agricultural land which produces outstanding crops of oats and barley, superb sheep and cattle, and top-quality seed potatoes.

Farmlands are surrounded by wonderful, heather-covered moorlands, although one is never far from the sound of the sea; and Orkney has been home and haven for wanderers for thousands of years. The earliest settlers left behind them a remarkable array of monuments: standing stones, burial chambers, villages and brochs.

Skara Brae, built before Egypt's Great Pyramid Age: ten Stone Age houses, uncovered by a sand storm in 1850. The stone circles at Brodgar and Stenness. Maes Howe Chambered Cairn, sealed by its priests more than 5,000 years ago; reopened and looted by Vikings in 1150 AD.

Norsemen conquered Orkney in the ninth century when the islands became dependencies of Norway and Denmark. It was during the time of Viking domination that Rognvald Kolsson began to build his magnificent, red sandstone cathedral in Kirkwall, named after martyred St Magnus, killed on the island of Eglisay in 1116 AD. It is said that, before he died, St Magnus asked his executioner to kill him by an axe stroke to the head, rather than suffer decapitation: "For it is not seemly to behead chiefs like thieves." When the remains of the saint were found in 1919, in a pillar in St Magnus Cathedral, the skull was deeply marked, by an axe-blow.

King Haakon, defeated by Alexander II of Scotland at the Battle of Largs in 1263, fled to Orkney, where he died later the same year; and Norse rule ended when King Christian I pledged Orkney as security for the dowry of his daughter, The Maid of Norway, sent as bride to King James III. The dowry was never paid and Orkney became part of Scotland.

Evidence of the stormy days of Viking rule abound, particularly on the island of Birsay, their fortress off the north-west coast of Mainland. The ruins of a great banqueting hall remain and, as boys, my brother and I refought many an imagined battle amongst the grey stones of Brough of Birsay.

We first visited Orkney in 1952, on a family holiday, and I suspect that experience had a lot to do with stimulating my love of islands. We sailed from Edinburgh's port of Leith, on the RMS *St Ninian*, and that journey was my first real adventure into the unknown.

The overnight passage to Aberdeen was wild and stormy and my brother Ian and I were amongst the few passengers on board capable of doing proper justice to the excellent dinner provided. Afterwards, we clung to the rail, listening to the wind howling; watching vast, angry waves crowding in on every side.

Mother and Father had retired hurt, along with my younger brother, Fergus, and they spent an unhappy night wrestling with the toils of sea-sickness. Stirred, white, green and shaken, they emerged the following morning to greet the new day.

We stopped for a few hours in Aberdeen, long enough to allow Father to take us to see the house we had lived in until 1939:

Stranathro, at Muchalls, perched high on the cliffs by the road to Stonehaven. Ian remembered it, but I didn't, being only a few months old at the time. However, it met with my instant approval: loud with the sound of waves and cry of gull.

The same afternoon, we sailed from Aberdeen to Kirkwall, blessed by calm seas and warm sunlight, chased by dolphin and myriad seabirds. I saw my first gannet, plunging into mirror-calm waters, snow-white, yellow-tipped bill ready to pounce on its prey sixty feet below the surface.

A long-tailed skua glided serenely overhead and I was entranced by its beauty. Although I had no idea then what species of bird it was, the picture was firmly fixed in my mind; years later I instantly recognised it in my first ornithological guide, P. A. D. Hollom's *The Popular Handbook of British Birds*.

My parents had rented a cottage on a farm at Backakeldy, ten miles south from Kirkwall overlooking the sea on the eastern shores of Scapa Flow. The farm was owned by three bachelor brothers and three spinster sisters. Senior brother, John Isbister, smiling brightly, met us at the pier. I instinctively knew I was going to like him.

Our cottage lay on stubby cliffs close by the sea. There was no road to it, or track, merely a worn path, two fields' distance from the farm; but to us, big city born and bred, it was magical, the stuff of which dreams are made, and for two weeks we lived a life of unadulterated bliss.

Outside the cottage door was a huge, ominous-looking shell which we were told had been fired from a battleship during World War I; and John pointed out to us exactly where the *Royal Oak* had been torpedoed in 1939. He said oil slicks from the stricken leviathan still sometimes marred the bay.

One of our greatest pleasures was collecting early morning provisions from the farm. We always found an excuse to linger round the milking parlour, warmed by the steaming animals; watching in admiration as one of the ladies coaxed milk from pink teats into a foaming bucket. An invitation to tea in the farmhouse kitchen was an almost unbearable delight; bright cinders glowed in the polished black stove; hot, freshly baked scones, butter, cheese, ten minute fresh eggs, milk from the sombre-eyed cows round the door; the scent of peat smoke, soothing all cares.

Like all Orcadians, the Isbisters were supremely gentle, kindly people, always with enough time to stop and talk to two excited small boys; and my life-long interest in birds was greatly encouraged by their patience and kindness.

One evening, as we stood talking by the shore, I saw a strange, beautifully shaped bird flying fast over the sea, rising in a long, slow arch, calling hauntingly as it flew. John told me that it was a red-throated diver; and those lovely creatures have remained favourites of mine ever since.

I also saw my first fulmar, sweeping the cliffs on stiff wings, endlessly gliding with miraculous ease; hen harrier haunted the moorlands; golden plover and curlew cried plaintively from banks of peat; statuesque heron stared balefully into shallow pools; widow-black cormorant dried their dark wings on seaweed-covered rocks. I became a bird watcher in Orkney.

We were allowed to help with the work of the farm, although more often than not I suspect we hindered the wheels of labour. In those days, horses were still used on many farms for ploughing and I soon found myself staggering red-faced up a furrow, furiously gripping the wooden handles, astonished at the power of the mighty beasts plodding sombrely ahead.

Ian, being older, was even luckier. He was allowed to drive the old red Ferguson tractor and one day we all crowded, laughing, aboard the trailer, to help the Isbisters bring home peat for winter fuel. The day we nearly lost young Fergus.

One minute he was there, the next gone, vanished from the face of the earth. I saw him disappear but, before I could say anything, Fergus started yelling. He had stumbled into a deep peat hole, hidden by heather, and worse, the heather had closed above his head, hiding where he had fallen.

John Isbister roared, "Keep yelling, son, I'm coming." He bounded across the moor, guided by Fergie's howls, and eventually discovered the spot. Parting the heather, he reached down and grabbed Fergus by the hand. With difficulty, John hauled my terrified brother to safety. Just in time. Fergus had been waist deep and sinking fast.

We had another narrow escape, and for years afterwards Father would go red with embarrassment when the subject was mentioned: "I must have been off my head," he would mutter ashamedly. The incident happened on the Churchill Barriers, the great concrete causeways Winston Churchill ordered to be built to protect the fleet in Scapa Flow from submarine attack, after the *Royal Oak* was sunk.

There are four causeways, from Mainland to Lamb Holm; Lamb Holm joining Glims Holm; Glims Holm to Burray; and Burray to South Ronaldsay. The Isbisters had lent Father their car and we spent the day exploring; visiting the Italian Chapel on Lamb Holm, built by Italian POWs, now guarded by a statue of St George; and the little hamlet of St Margaret's Hope.

Ian and I were particularly impressed with the half-submerged hulks of the Imperial German Navy, scuttled by their crews on 21 June 1919, after the First World War. We were both young enough and old enough to have vivid wartime memories of the Second World War, and were fascinated by the ominous array of masts and dark shapes in the bay.

The peace treaty ending the First World War remained unsigned by Germany six months after the eleventh hour of the eleventh day in the eleventh month of 1918. Rear-Admiral von Reuter, anticipating renewed conflict, commanded his fleet of seventy-two ships to be either scuttled or beached. As SMS *Hindenberg* went down, the German Ensign was lowered; and this flag may still be seen in the German Fleet Exhibition in Stromness.

But, after a glorious day's exploring, by the time we turned for home the weather had become very wild, and as we approached the first barrier, waves were breaking fiercely over the road. Nothing daunted, Father continued, in spite of protests from Mother.

Matters grew worse by the minute as Father pressed on, windscreen wipers working furiously. Waves flew over the car. How we survived remains a mystery, but when we eventually arrived at Backakeldy, we were told that the coastguard had been alerted and that our mad passage across the barriers had been watched in amazement by worried would-be rescuers.

Orkney casts a magic spell that never fades. People return again and again to these precious shores. After I married, we took our family across the broken waters of the Pentland Firth to spend a fishing holiday in a caravan by the shores of Loch Boardhouse.

Orcadian game fishing is of outstanding quality, both for wild brown trout and for sea-trout, most of which are caught in the sea off the northern shores of the Island of Hoy: Burra Sound, Chalmers Hope, Rysa Sound, Gutter Sound, Longhope and

North Bay. The best brown trout lochs are on Mainland: Harray, Stenness, Boardhouse, Hundland and Swannay. There are many others, all with their own special appeal, both on Mainland and amongst the other islands, but most anglers confine their activities to these five; and rarely regret their decision to do so.

Our caravan at Boardhouse was perfectly situated within casting distance of the loch, and we soon had the children, Blair and Lewis-Ann, lashing away like old hands. Each evening, after supper, Ann and I would launch the boat and fish the long summer night, accompanied by the sound of curlew and ghostly shape of long-eared owl; and happy splash of rising trout.

We revisited the scenes of my childhood, fighting old battles on Birsay, wandering round the tumbled stones of Skara Brae, then still undeveloped and free from tourist organisation. The beach at Skara Brae, the Bay of Skail, is one of the loveliest in Scotland: half a mile of yellow sand, washed by endless, white-fringed, green Atlantic waves.

Orkney waters are warmed by the Gulf Streams and we often swam at Skail. I taught my first dog, a shy golden retriever named Jean, to swim there. She showed a distinctively un-retriever-like fear of water, so eventually I carried her out and set her afloat. She swam happily ever after.

Years later, when we came to live in Caithness, with two more children in the clan, we visited Orkney frequently. The rough passage from Scrabster was a small price to pay and three hours after leaving home, we could be fishing, or stalking the wild cliffs.

Harray is the principal trout fishery, producing upwards of 20,000 trout each year. It is an exciting loch, not only because of the quality of trout, but also because of its varied nature. There are dozens of attractive bays round the shore; skerries, underwater rocky outcrops, lie scattered throughout its six-mile length; knowing where they are is all important.

Bank fishing can be just as productive as fishing from a boat, so even during the high winds that are your frequent companion on Orkney, anglers can always find a sheltered corner from which to attack. The heaviest trout taken from Harray was a magnificent fish weighing 17lb 8oz, caught in 1964, and trout of over 4lb in weight are still taken most seasons.

Boats are readily available to visitors, from various mooring bays around Harray, but my favourite venue is the Merkister Hotel, at

15

the north-east end of the loch; a true fishing hotel, to which anglers return, year after year; where fishermen new to Orkney are given expert advice and endless encouragement.

Loch of Stenness lies adjacent to Harray, separated from it by a narrow strip of moorland dominated by the Ring of Brodgar. Orkney's largest trout was caught in Stenness and this mighty fish weighed 29lb 8oz. Today, this dramatic loch still produces superb trout of unequalled quality; and sea-trout, fresh from the tide that races through the outlet at Bridge of Waithie into Bay of Ireland and Hoy Sound.

But the most dramatic monument is the Standing Stones of Stenness. Three of the grey slabs stand more than fifteen feet high and the setting is superb. Southwards, the gentle hills of Hoy crowd the horizon; northwards lies Loch of Stenness, bobbed white with graceful mute swans, shores edged emerald and gold with seaweed.

In 1967, my wife Ann made a drawing of Stenness, including a stone bench across two stubby, central columns. Twenty years later, viewing a contemporary photograph of the Standing Stones, I noticed that the cross-slabs had gone. I complained mightily, only to be told that the stone table was a well-intentioned after-thought, erected in recent times, and that it had been removed to restore the henge to its original form. But I still miss Ann's stone.

Although Orkney fishing is advertised as being free, most visitors join the Orkney Trout Fishing Association for the duration of their holiday. The charge is modest and money collected is used to improve fishing and facilities. Members have the use of Association mooring bays, jetties and fishing huts; and the sure and certain knowledge that they are supporting the very best of causes: their own future pleasure and enjoyment.

One Easter, we rented a cottage in Sandwick. In spite of fierce, cold weather we decided to assault my favourite Orkney loch, Swannay. Fighting our way through a raging snowstorm, we arrived at the north end, by Costa Hill, and huddled in the car, astonished by the force of the blizzard.

Ann, made of sterner stuff than the rest of her tribe, leapt from the car, determined to fish. Within moments of setting off, she was lost from view, swallowed up in the white mist. We waited, wondering whether or not to follow. After twenty minutes, I glimpsed her figure, red hat and green coat, shoulders bent, struggling back, snowwoman-like — with a superb trout weighing 2lb.

The next morning we returned to Swannay, by Dale Farm. April sunlight sparkled over the water, dancing across snow-covered fields. As a gesture, rather than with serious intent, I bank fished. Within moments I had hooked and landed two of the most perfect brown trout that I have ever caught, each weighing about 1lb 8oz.

That night, we cooked and ate the Swannay trout for supper. Then, with wind howling round the windows and rattling the doors, we sat in front of a peat fire and played games with the children. The following year, Blair and Lewis-Ann were off, chasing their own, adult fortunes. But the memory of that last family holiday together in Orkney lingers forever.

ALTNAHARRA

**INGING** is the secret of fishing success. Persuading trout to rise has nothing whatsoever to do with weather conditions, casting technique or the selection of flies. It has to do with music.

Orpheus understood this. Creatures crowded round to hear him sing. Whether or not Orpheus was an angler, I don't know, but I do know that when all else fails, giving them a song always works.

This may sound fanciful, but believe me, it is true. I know what I am talking about. Or rather singing about. It has happened too often to me to be mere coincidence. If trout are not rising, or fishing conditions seem impossible, I hum a tune. Sure enough, within a few moments, up they come.

If you don't believe me, ask David MacGregor Aird, expert Edinburgh angler and good friend. We were fishing together recently on Plantation Loch, near Altnaharra in North-West Sutherland, catching nothing. Grasping courage in both lips, I explained my musical theorem.

"You must be joking, Bruce!" he exclaimed. "Pull the other one." I persisted. "Give it a try, David, no one else need ever know, and it really does work." We fished on in silence, still catching nothing. So I decided to use my most potent song: the aria from Handel's *Messiah*, "He shall feed his flock".

Handel wrote the *Messiah* in London, where he lived in a house close to present-day King's Cross Station, five years after suffering

18

a severe stroke, and it received its first performance in Dublin in 1742. I discovered the *Messiah* when I was sixteen years old and I was overwhelmed by the sheer beauty and grandeur of Handel's enduring masterpiece.

One August evening I was fishing the Tweed at Manor, downstream from where Manor Water bustles in from the south to meet the "Queen" of Scottish rivers. There is a large, calm pool, below the bridge; then the river narrows, rushing quickly through a rapid stream into a broad, smooth run. At the end of this run the river strikes a high bank and swirls into a deep, clear pool, before swinging right and left, on under the old railway bridge, down towards Neidpath Castle. I was certain I would catch something in Rock Pool, and my hopes mounted as I waded silently to the perfect casting position.

I caught nothing. Saw nothing. I was beginning to think that I would be going home fishless when I found myself singing, "He shall feed his flock"; and fell to musing upon how well I would be able to feed five, let alone five thousand, given the reluctance of the fish to show even a snout above the surface.

Almost instantly as I sang, a trout rose and grabbed my tail fly, a size 16 Silver Butcher. I landed him, gratefully, and carried on fishing, and singing. The very next cast, another fish rose, was hooked and landed. With the prospect of action in sight, I remained silent, concentrating on casting. Nothing. But the moment I started singing again, I caught another trout. Six fish later, I called it a day; thanked the good Lord for his kindness, strapped the creel to the back of my motor bike, and roared triumphantly home.

David Aird jumped in alarm as I burst into song, rocking the boat dangerously. "For heaven's sake Bruce, have you gone stark, raving mad?" Two seconds later, I was into a good fish and soon had the trout in the net and into the boat. David looked in astonishment.

"Go on, David, try." Red-faced and embarrassed, Mr Aird cleared his throat and launched into a few bars from Jean Sibelius *Finlandia*. Immediately, a trout rose and grabbed his bob fly. "Would you believe it?" he exclaimed; and for the next ten minutes the surrounding hills were alive with the sound of music, and the happy splash of rising trout.

For a number of years, my wife Ann and I have been fishing

with a party of friends at Altnaharra. We call ourselves "The Naver Nuts", given our strenuous, and more often than not, unproductive attempts to remove salmon, and anything else that moves, from this six-mile-long, dour, windy water. The basket of trout David and I displayed from Plantation Loch aroused considerable interest among our companions; and we were soon being closely questioned about what flies had done the damage. That night, at dinner, David and I came clean, and told our friends about singing to fish.

Incredulity greeted this explanation. For the next hour we silently suffered their ribald comments and downright abuse. A prerequisite of being a member of our party is a thick skin and a sense of humour. Having a sense of humour is probably more important than having a fishing rod amongst "The Naver Nuts".

The following evening, when everyone returned to the hotel, quite a few fish had been caught, even a couple of Naver salmon. "What did they take, Ron?" I inquired politely. "Promise you won't tell, Bruce, but actually, it was Beethoven's *Fifth Piano Concerto*. The slow movement did the trick," he replied.

For the rest of the week, each morning, when tactics were discussed prior to setting out, the talk was not of Goat's Toe, Garry Dog or Grouse & Claret. It was: "Have you tried Schuman yet? I had two beauties on the *Spring Symphony*." "No, it's a Johann Sebastian day. I think I will give them a *Brandenburg Concerto*."

Altnaharra is a comfortable fishing hotel at the head of Loch Naver. Charles Maclaren used to run his fishing course there and a devoted band of anglers return each year to battle with salmon and sea-trout in Naver, Mallart and Loch Hope; or to enjoy marvellous trout fishing in the lochs scattered throughout the hills.

Recently, I was given a copy of an old book, *A guide to the Fishing Inns of Scotland*, by R. Crombie Saunders, one-time editor of *The Scottish Angler*, and published in 1951. At that time Altnaharra Hotel had seventeen miles of river fishing and charged £1 for every salmon caught. Accommodation rates were £9.9s per week, full board. Dinner cost 5s. Happy days.

The hotel lies amidst superb scenery. Scotland at its finest. Two Munros, 3,000-foot peaks, are available for pre-breakfast exercise: Ben Klibreck (3,154 feet), overlooking Loch Naver, and Ben Hope (3,040 feet), towering above lovely Loch Hope. Both are easy, rewarding climbs with magnificent panoramas from their summits. Westwards, range after range of blue hills and mountains crowd the horizon: Ben Stack, Arkle, Foinaven, Ganu Mor, Cranstackie; and a distant prospect of the "Heather Isle" of Lewis, in the Outer Hebrides, shimmering and dancing in Atlantic haze.

To the south, beyond Ben Hee, the sharp point of Quinag rears above Glen Coul; mighty Ben More Assynt, the highest peak in Sutherland; Canisp, Suilven and, on a clear day, the mountains of Fisherfield and Flowerdale Forests: An Teallach, by Destitution Road, and Slioch, the Spear, guarding Loch Maree.

East and north, vast Flow Country peatlands sparkle blue and silver with lochs and lochans. Caithness mountains, Morven and Scaraben, rise from the level moor. Across the Pentland Firth, leaden-grey Atlantic and North Sea waves wash gentle Orkney Isles, dominated by Ward Hill on red-cliffed Hoy.

My first glimpse of Strathnaver came shortly after Crombie Saunders' guide appeared, in 1955, on a family holiday. Father had booked accommodation with Mrs Mackay, at Skail; a lady of rigid Presbyterian principals, but also, it was alleged, not above netting the River Naver, which flowed conveniently past her back door.

The dominant memory I have of Skail, however, is not of psalm-singing Mrs Mackay, but of her porridge, dished up each morning with malignant glee. The best way to test the quality of porridge is to throw it at the wall. That which clings, momentarily, then slithers down is deemed useless. Genuinely constructed porridge should knock a hole straight through. In this respect, Mrs Mackay's mixture was outstanding.

From the dawn of history, men have lived and worked in Strathnaver. The first settlers, displaced from central Europe by forces unknown, probably because they couldn't pay some Mesolithic Poll Tax, trekked north with their women and children, building circular huts amidst sea-shore sand dunes. Little remains to mark their passing other than small artifacts, found in the middens of their daily life.

Their descendants left more enduring memorials: magnificent burial chambers, massive structures, involving placing hundreds of tons of carefully shaped stones. These graves were built to house the remains of important members of the tribe, and one of the most notable lies close to Mrs Mackay's old home at Skail: a polygonal chamber, with several stone slabs which still hint at the original character of this round cairn.

The most spectacular Strathnaver monuments are the brochs which zig-zag up the River Naver, from the sea at Invernaver, to Mudale, south from Altnaharra; huge, circular, fortified towers, forty feet high, enclosing an inner court some fifty feet in diameter, with double walls, fifteen feet thick, containing galleries and stairs, and windows facing inwards.

These Iron Age structures were built before the arrival of the Vikings; but why they were built, or who their architects feared, remains a mystery to this day. My own theory is that then, like now, it was a convenient way to discourage unwanted visitors: "Dad," the call would come from the top of the tower, "I can see Mother-in-law and Auntie Bessie coming up the hill." The door could be quickly locked and peace preserved.

The Romans never subdued these northern, painted men, the Picts; nor did war-like Vikings, plundering down the strath in search of food, treasure and slaves; and as King Malcolm struggled to unite his fractious kingdom, Clan Mackay in Strathnaver pursued their independent, Highland way; tending black cattle, growing sparse crops, squabbling happily amongst themselves and their Caithness neighbours.

So-called civilisation arrived in Sutherland in the nineteenth century, after the clan system had been destroyed by the disastrous machinations of Prince Charles Edward Stewart, Bonnie Prince Charlie. His defeat at Culloden in 1746 ushered in a fearsome era of repression and violent change in the North; and nowhere was this new order felt more savagely than in nineteenth-century Strathnaver. It was the "time of the sheep", and to make way for these white settlers, people had to go. The Highland Clearances.

The work of eviction in Strathnaver was carried out between 1809 and 1819 by Patrick Seller, land agent and factor to Elizabeth, Countess Duchess of Sutherland, and her husband, the Marquess of Stafford, one of the richest men in Europe. Stafford's Sutherland estates produced an annual income of £16,000, but this was not enough. It was decided that by clearing the people and turning the land over to Lowland sheep farmers, income would be much increased.

Stafford, who sometimes spent £16,000 in a single day on antiques at Christie's sales in London, was never troubled by his conscience. James Loch, Edinburgh lawyer and Commissioner for Stafford's Sutherland estates, reassured his master that: "The adoption of the new system, by which the mountainous districts are converted into sheep pastures, even if it should unfortunately occasion the emigration of some individuals, is, upon the whole, advantageous to the nation at large."

Fifteen thousand men, women and children where ruthlessly evicted from their homes and Patrick Seller was well rewarded for his evil work: by 1819, he rented no less than 75,000 acres of cleared land, and lived in grand style in a fine house at Syre — ruling dispossessed Clan Mackay with an iron, heartless hand.

The clearances began in April 1814, at the village of Grumore, on the banks of Loch Naver. All that remains now of the sixteen dwellings Seller burned are a few tumbled stones, scattered over the green hillside. George MacDonald saw the people from Strathnaver arriving at the sea: "When they came down from the Strath to the sea-shore they suffered very much from want of houses. They hurriedly threw up earthen walls, stretching blankets over the top to shelter them; and cooped up in a small place like this, four or five families together, they spent the following winter."

The horror of the Strathnaver clearances was eventually exposed by Donald Macleod, who as a young boy had been evicted by Seller from the village of Rossal. His book, *Gloomy Memories of the Highlands*, was a strident counter-blast to Harriet Beacher Stowe's volume, *Happy Memories of Foreign Lands*, which included a glowing account of many acts of kindness the Duke and Duchess of Sutherland had bestowed upon their people. A memorial to Macleod stands by the side of the river, close to the site of his old home.

A few miles south from Bettyhill, named after the infamous Countess Duchess of Sutherland, is another notable Strathnaver memorial. It is a stone commemorating the place where one of Britain's most famous infantry regiments was raised, the 93rd Sutherlandshire Highlanders. During the wars with France at the turn of the nineteenth century, when the call came, more than 2,000 Highlanders volunteered for service with the colours. Two hundred and fifty came from Strathnaver and 104 of them had the same surname: William Mackay. During a time of harsh military discipline, when drum-head courts, public floggings and hangings were carried out to "encourage the rest", the 93rd were excused from attendance at show-piece parades; because not a single member of their regiment was ever punished. Highland pride.

Other battles are still fought today in Strathnaver, but they are between man and beast, rather than between man and his fellow creatures. The River Naver is one of the finest salmon streams in Scotland and each year hundreds of salmon are caught from its peat-stained waters.

Obtaining permission to fish, however, is another matter. The river is a jealously guarded preserve and very expensive. Recently, the Syre Beat was sold for a sum believed to be well in excess of £3m, and there was no shortage of bidders; including, it is said, the heir to Britain's throne.

However, at the mouth of the river, in the tidal and estuary waters, fishing is often available to casual visitors, and sport can be excellent, particularly with sea-trout.

When we stayed at Skail, Father and I fished the mouth of the river, with our customary skill. I caught nothing, but lost my favourite fishing hat, whisked from my head during a great wind that made casting almost impossible. At least, that was my excuse for not catching anything.

With the exception of the River Naver, fishing opportunities abound at Altnaharra and the only real problem is knowing where to begin. During our last visit, Ann and I, and our oldest son, Blair, walked out to fish a series of delightful trout lochs to the south-east of Loch Loyal. It was a splendid, memorable day, walking, fishing and simply lazing in warm June sunlight, lulled by the song of lark and meadow pipit.

Loch Tarvie, to the north of Loch Naver, is another of our favourites; an hour's gentle walk from the road, deep into the hills, past ruined shielings to utter paradise.

Tarvie trout fight like fury and are beautifully marked with bright red spots; and in this delightful little loch there are some excellent fish which can almost pull the rod from your hand in their first mad rush.

But of all Altnaharra fishing, Loch Hope offers the most spectacular sport. Hope has a magical quality that instantly ensnares. The setting is superb. A long, silver sword of water, knifing through a dark glen, crowded round by majestic hills: Ben Hope to the east, Feinne-bheinn Mhor, Meall Glas and An Leancharn westwards.

Because of its narrow shape, six miles in length, north to south, Hope can be very windy. Indeed, sometimes it is impossible to launch a boat, and anglers should treat Loch Hope with great respect. Always wear a life-jacket when afloat.

The first time I fished Hope was with Alan Finch, a previous owner of Altnaharra Hotel. Alan, whom I didn't know very well, had invited Ann and me over for the day, and had also offered to act as our gillie. This was too good an opportunity to miss because Alan had fished Hope for many years and knew every inch, intimately.

Writing about fishing, as I do, brings problems. People imagine that just because you write about fishing, you are also an expert angler. Which I most certainly am not, as nearest and dearest, and gangs of so-called friends will confirm. Like everyone else, I do my best, try very hard, and leave a lot to luck. No expert.

However, I am expected to maintain the image of an angling guru, and all too frequently this uncomfortable mask slips; generally leaving me red-faced with embarrassment, furiously attempting to devise some semi-acceptable excuse for rampant stupidity or lack of skill. It was the same with our local village cricket team. Just because I had a bat and had played at school, they assumed I was some kind of expert. In fact, at school my cricket nickname was "First-ball Bruce". I was invariably out first throw.

So when we arrived hopefully at Loch Hope that morning, I was on my best behaviour. Determined not to put a foot wrong, let alone go in over the top, as I sometimes do.

I asked Alan to fish the first drift, in order to settle down, and towards the end he suggested that I put up the dap. My heart sank. I had never touched a real dapping-rod in my life, and Alan's was telescopic, extending to seventeen feet in length. Put this up, in a small boat, in a force five gale?

I struggled manfully for a few minutes, neatly nicking Ann's fishing hat off, which we had to row after to recover; catching Alan's flies, on a back cast, and finally managing to get floss and line mixed up in an unbelievably intricate tangle. How Alan kept his temper I will never know, but he quietly sorted out the mess, mounted a huge Loch Ordie, rowed out from the shore again and handed me the fly rod: "Here, Bruce, you fish, I'll work the dap and mind the oars." Blushing, I grabbed the proffered rod, carefully avoiding Ann's look of resignation, and instantly hooked both the dap and Ann's cast at the same time.

The wind had risen, blowing the boat ever faster shorewards, and, as Alan wrestled with the oars, I tried to unfankle the heap of floss and flies, catching my tail fly on the bottom of the boat in the process. "No problem, Bruce, I'll beach the boat." Ashore, Alan hunted round the hull, searching for the stuck fly, getting both arms and half a leg wet whilst doing so. By this time, I am sure he was convinced that he was afloat with a lunatic.

It is hard to find things to say at times like these and, "Don't know what's wrong with me today. Never happened before," didn't seem appropriate. So I shut up, suffered, and carried on fishing. We fished for several hours without seeing so much as a fin. Alan insisted upon managing the oars, which made it even worse. I sensed him thinking that we should have had half a dozen in the boat by now.

Quietly, under my breath, I began humming Handel. If Alan heard, he remained silent, probably resolving to get ashore as quickly as possible. The first fish grabbed seconds later, and after a considerable struggle was safely landed. Three more followed, in quick succession. Thank God for Handel, I thought, with four sea-trout weighing 10lb: "Come on Alan," I said, "this is hardly fair. Why don't you have a cast? There seem to be fish about after all."

NORTHUMBERLAND

I WAS born and brought up in Edinburgh during the days when Scotland's capital merited its ancient title, "Auld Reekie". The reason for this name was obvious from the top of Arthur's Seat in King's Park: the town's spires and towers were half-glimpsed shapes, shimmering murkily through the pall of smoke that covered the city.

But when I returned from military service in 1960, my employers asked me to represent them south of the border, in that troutless land beyond Mr Hadrian's Wall known as England. At first I demurred. What, give up my glorious Scottish game fishing? Never see my native land again, mountains, moorlands and glens, apart from brief holiday excursions?

Eventually, I succumbed, resigning myself to my fate. And thus, happily, I discovered Yorkshire and Northumberland. Surely two of Britain's most beautiful counties. At first, however, we lived in County Durham, in the new town of Peterlee, until then but a strange name briefly glimpsed on packets of Tudor Crisps. East Durham was very much a mining community; and as my wife found, a prerequisite for employment was a fully paid-up, current Labour Party membership card. But in time, we came to admire the people of the drab County Durham towns: Houghton-le-Springs, Hetton-le-Hole, Easington, Horden, Blackhall Colliery, Wheatly and Shotton; grouped around their incongruous, magnificent capital, Durham City.

We found a neat village south of Peterlee called Elwick, complete with tree-decked, green, Tabatha Twitchet shop and two super pubs, where we lived uneasily for three years. Ann worked in British West Hartlepool: severely shelled during World War I, home of Andy Cap and where they hung a shipwrecked monkey in Napoleonic times, in the belief that the poor beast was a Frenchman.

The nearest I came to fishing was as number three in a racing four on the grubby River Tees, when I joined the Tees Amateur Rowing Club. Not much rose on the Tees at Stockton in those days, least of all trout; and a ducking was followed by a dash to hospital and an appointment with a stomach pump. The Tees is much improved now, but then it was virtually an open sewer.

When we heard of the decision to construct a new reservoir on the Durham/Northumberland border, Ann and I carefully noted opening day in our diary; and on the appointed morning we rose at dawn and sallied forth, bustling by ash-covered Consett Iron Works, the light of battle glinting in our trout-starved eyes.

Within twenty minutes of arrival, we had both caught the prescribed limit; strange, stump-tailed rainbow trout that threw themselves instantly at whatever fly we offered. We sat on the bank, dejected, wondering what we would have to do to find "proper" trout fishing, such as we had been brought up with in our native land.

We fished Derwent fairly frequently for the following two years, and in time, found pleasure in doing so. The trout settled into their new habitat and became relatively wild, dour and more discriminating, some growing to considerable size.

I vividly remember our last visit. We had taken a London business colleague out who had never fished before; the sort of man who had done everything and knew everything. Ann and I laboured mightily to no avail. Our friend from the smoke, vigorously lashing away like a cab driver whipping a lazy horse, caught three.

Towards evening, as a fine mist began to settle on the water, we drifted into a bay at the east end of the reservoir. On the bank, stood a small man, dressed in a stained old raincoat, wearing a flat cap, fishing tackle packed in an ex-army gas-mask carrier. His rod was an ex-army tank aerial with an ancient, creaking brass reel. As we watched, peering through the mist, he hooked an enormous fish which almost pulled the rod from out of his hands. He staggered back, gripping the rod furiously as the trout tore off to the depths. I can still hear his plaintiff cry, in a strong Durham accent, before the cast broke: "He's pulling al me line oot."

Alternative fishing and help came from a most unexpected quarter, in the shape of a book by Anya Seaton called *Devil Water*; a marvellous historical novel by a master story-teller, describing the tragic, romantic life of James Radcliffe, Earl of Derwentwater, and his younger brother Charles, both executed for their support of the Jacobite cause during the revolutions of 1715 and 1745.

The Radcliffes lived at Dilston Hall, by Devil Water, a tributary of the Tyne that joins the main river near Hexham. We made a pilgrimage to Dilston, wandering round the ruined, ivy-clad tower and were utterly captivated by the beauty of Hexhamshire and determined to move north as quickly as possible.

The house we found stood on a hill amidst fine old elm trees, looking south over the Tyne Valley and River South Tyne, midway between the villages of Bardon Mill and Haltwhistle. Built during the seventeenth century, our new home was reputed to have been the birthplace of one of Northumberland's most famous sons: Nicholas Ridley, Bishop of London.

Bishop Ridley was burned at the stake along with Hugh Latimer outside Oxford in 1555, during the reign of Bloody Mary. The wood used for the fire was green and new. Consequently, it produced more smoke than flames and Ridley cried out in pain. His sterner companion comforted him: "Play the man Master Ridley. We shall light such a fire today in England that, by God's grace, it will never be put out."

It took the sad pair a long time to burn — I once read that the bill for the execution, including stake, chains and timber, came to about £3.7s.6d, a not inconsiderable sum in those days; but Hugh Latimer was right: the fire of their religious conviction was never extinguished.

I soon found myself engrossed in the history of the valley; tales and stories of the turbulent times of Border wars. There was always unrest along the Border line; during the Scottish Wars of Independence, the English Civil War, religious wars, in fact most of the time; and of course, if Border lairds were not involved in a national dispute, then there were always plenty of old scores to be settled to keep them gainfully employed.

29

But best of all, I found myself gainfully employed in the South Tyne, which was only a ten-minute walk from the front door, five if I ran, which I often did. The first items unpacked were trout-rods; and they stayed up, ready and waiting for instant use for as long as we lived there.

My great fishing love, until then, had been Lady Tweed, but I soon discovered the South Tyne was every bit as good, if not better, than the Queen of Scottish rivers; and the stretch below our house was far enough upstream and far enough downstream from the main population centres to make it almost completely private.

In the seven years we lived there, only once did I ever meet another fisherman on my favourite part of the river; and over the years I came to know the South Tyne and its wildlife as well as Mole or Rat in *Wind and the Willows* ever knew their water. And loved it every bit as much as they adored their riverside home.

The South Tyne Valley also offered splendid walking possibilities. Our house was close to Hadrian's Wall and a favourite outing was to Whinshields Crag, the highest point. The Romans started building their wall in about 122 AD and upon completion it ran from Wallsend-on-Tyne in the east to Bowness on Solway in the west, a distance of seventy-three miles.

Housteads, eight-and-a-half miles west of Chollerford, is the best preserved fort along the wall: five acres in extent and once accommodating 1,000 infantry. Walls, gateways, headquarter buildings and granaries can still be seen.

A few miles south, Vindolanda was the home of 500 Roman auxiliary soldiers. We used to explore the site when it was still a group of undeveloped grassy mounds. Now, a full-scale replica of part of the Roman Wall has been erected; there is a museum, listening posts, video programmes, picnic and toilet facilities — and thousands of visitors.

The Roman Wall was built as much to keep people in, as to keep the wild tribes from the north out. The wall delineated the northernmost frontier of Roman civilisation. The Picts could see for themselves the benefits and in doing so, the Romans hoped, would cease their war-like activities and come to heel. They never did.

Much of the Roman Wall was spirited away by local farmers; the old stones were ideal for building into house and byre. Indeed,

30

even in our own garden, in the centre of a rose bed, there was a small slab which looked suspiciously Roman; I am sure in the dim and distant past it had been filched from the wall.

From Hadrian's Wall there are spectacular views northwards, over Kielder Forest to the Cheviots; and, for the angler, closer to hand, spectacular views of three excellent trout lochs lying at the foot of Steel Rigg, one of the most dramatic sections of the wall: Broomlee, Greenlee and Crag Loughs.

In spite of their proximity, I never managed to fish these lochs. Angling was controlled by a private club with a long waiting list. I applied for membership, but the day approval finally arrived, four years later, was the day we left the valley.

However, I never really worried too much about the Crag Loughs, because there was so much wonderful sport to be had elsewhere, on both river and loch. Even in those days, the South Tyne had good runs of salmon and we often stood by the weir at Haltwhistle in September, watching salmon fighting their way upstream.

The Tyne was heavily polluted, from about Prudhoe down to the sea, but after rain, salmon swam upstream in the clean water on top of the flood. Now, major sewage interceptor schemes have been completed and the Tyne is undoubtedly the finest salmon stream in England; and getting better every year.

Yellow flies were most popular with Tyne trout, and the best fish I took weighed 2lb, although a few much heavier trout escaped my evil intent. Being in the right place at the right time is all important in fishing, and living on the doorstep of the river gave me the advantage. Providing fresh trout for dinner was rarely a problem.

Allen Water, a major tributary of the South Tyne, offered perfect dry fly fishing. Difficult, delicate work, because the small stream is heavily wooded; but the trout are of excellent quality and, although rarely very large, fight surprisingly well.

The woods surrounding Allen were also a favourite for family walks; marvellous old trees, oak, ash, sycamore, beech, elm and chestnut, nodding in the breeze; the forest floor was carpeted with flowers, spring bluebell and primrose beckoning us on; summer squirrel darted through the branches and the air was full of the scent of wild garlic; red and brown autumn leaves ushered in winters that dressed our world sparkling white.

Our local pub, the Wallace Arms, run by Ted and Brenda Roper, was about three miles from Haltwhistle, close to Fetherstone Castle; a fine, red sandstone structure overlooking the South Tyne and still occupied. Fetherstone was used as a POW camp during the last World War, and the ruins of the camp's huts still litter parklands by the river.

The only German prisoner ever to escape from Britain, described in the book *The One that Got Away*, made his first attempt from Fetherstone. Pretending to be a Polish airman, he almost flew off from Carlisle with one of Britain's newest fighter planes before his true identity was discovered.

Walking through the camp during autumn months, I used to feel the presence of these long-departed prisoners; their laughter and despair and the harsh commands of their captors. Often, we would disturb huge salmon, red-dressed for spawning, and I suspect that during the days of the POW camp, salmon were a frequent supplement to meagre wartime rations.

Catcleugh Reservoir, just south of Carter Bar, was another favourite venue. This was also controlled by a private club, but we were sometimes given a day's fishing and generally managed to come home with a few trout. Catcleugh was stocked with a Loch Leven strain of fish, pink-fleshed, which were splendid fun to catch and always fought furiously.

Another furious fight took place not far from Catcleugh in 1388, the midnight Battle of Otterburn. James, Earl of Douglas, raided Northumberland, laying siege to Newcastle, and after a few days' inconclusive skirmishing, the Scots army retreated into the Cheviot Hills. "Henry Hotspur", son of the Earl of Northumberland pursued them and, as night fell on 5 August, surprised the Scots army encamped near Otterburn in Redesdale.

The battle raged throughout the moon-bright night and although the Scots were heavily outnumbered, they eventually won the day; however, during the fight, Douglas was brought to the ground by three spear wounds. As he lay dying, a kinsman, Sir John Sinclair, asked how he did: "Right evil, cousin, but thanked be God there hath been but few of mine ancestors that hath died in their beds." The news of the death of their leader was concealed from the Scots and Sinclair hoisted the Douglas banner and drove the English from the field.

I was nourished on stories like these; William Wallace, slaying half a dozen English soldiers with his fishing rod; Bruce, before Bannockburn, felling an English knight with one stroke from his slender battle-axe; and when I was a boy I contracted a mortal dread of dying in bed. To my young mind it seemed a most unScottish thing to do. People would obviously conclude that I had died a coward.

Near the site of the fight, present-day battles still take place; but between man and fish, rather than Scots and English. There is a very lovely lough close by called Sweethope, a classic place to fish; calm and sheltered, surrounded by mature trees; well managed, not very deep and full of splendid trout.

When we first fished Sweethope in 1973, it was owned by Vaux Breweries, Sunderland, and managed by a retired naval officer who lived in a house by the side of the lough. Anglers received a warm welcome and his lounge, overlooking the water, was packed with fishing books and there was always a table covered with the feathers and hooks of fly-tying.

What I most admired, was the direct access from the upper level to the boathouse, neatly situated below the lounge; to me, the pinnacle of achievement in house design. Up in the morning and, seconds later, into your first fish.

Sweethope has become an excellent put-and-take fishery and there are two loughs: Great Lough and Little Lough. Little Lough was created in the early eighteenth century by damming the stream that is the source of the River Wansbeck, and Great Lough was formed in 1850, immediately upstream. Both waters are surrounded by mature Scots pine and Sweethope Loughs appear entirely natural today. They are regularly stocked with rainbow and brown trout, and fish of up to 6lb 12 oz have been caught in recent years.

The present incumbent of my dream house is Mr F. D. H. Roe, Fishery Manager, who maintains the friendly traditions of his predecessor, offering useful advice to visitors regarding fishing techniques.

I found that a traditional Scottish technique often brought splendid results, particularly in calm conditions. The tall pines surrounding the lough often produced a mirror-like surface, and whilst it was easier to see rising fish, it was almost impossible to tempt them to take a fly, no matter how carefully presented.

It was then that the art of the "turning flee" came into its own.

The boat is rowed slowly round the lough whilst an angler sitting in the stern casts out at right angles. The flies are allowed to settle on the surface and are left to their own devices. The forward movement of the boat eventually turns the flies; and it is generally just as the flies begin to turn that a fish will take. All the angler has to do is raise the point of his rod, and the fish hooks itself. Our best calm day using this method produced a basket of six fish weighing 7lb.

There are many more exciting game-fishing opportunities awaiting the angler in Northumberland; and the Northumberland Water Authority publish an informative guide to help the visiting angler find sport. Unlike Scotland, a Water Authority Rod Licence is required in England, prior to fishing, as well as a permit from the water chosen.

All the loughs and reservoirs are stocked and the most productive, such as Grassholme, Hury and Fontburn, see upwards of 10,000 trout taken each season. Kielder Water, the largest man-made reservoir in Europe, surrounded by the largest man-made forest in Europe, was opened by HM The Queen in June 1982, and has been developed into a major water-sports centre.

Kielder offers a wide range of recreational opportunities. You may launch your own sailing dinghy, motor cruiser or canoe; there are facilities for swimming, water-skiing and sub-aqua diving. The Forestry Commission have laid out walks and trails with viewpoints and there are guided tours organised from two information centres. Forest drives and pony trekking are also available. The Boy Scouts and YMCA both have centres at Kielder and the entire twenty-seven-mile shoreline is open to trout anglers, with fishing boats waiting for hire at Matthew's Linn. You are never alone at Kielder.

But I remember Kielder Valley before it was flooded, when it was but a gleam in the developer's eye; and I remember the futile protests and the sadness of the communities who lost their homes.

We were told that the water was required to serve an expected expansion of industrial activity on Teesside. The predicted expansion never came and it may be argued that Kielder, and the flooding of the valley, was a disastrous example of the worst kind of crystal-ball gazing so frequently employed to force unwelcome developments on an unwilling population; and once again, the experts got it wrong.

I often wonder what happens to these faceless experts. Are they ever sacked, or disciplined for their blunders? Or do they just move on, looking for fresh fields and pastures new to flood?

We left Northumberland in 1975, to move north to Caithness, taking with us many happy memories of our time in the beautiful valley of the South Tyne; but I also took something more tangible, which reminds me of Northumberland every time I use it: my present trout-rod.

It is a fine, built-cane rod, made by Mr Stott, a retired employee of Hardy Brother's, Alnwick. Mr Stott's workshop was actually on the Roman Wall and every time I cast, or see my rod bend in anger, I am reminded of my beautiful Northumberland home.

SCOURIE

HE further north and west you go, the more lochs you see; and there are places in the far north where lochs and lochans outnumber people. A few years ago a friend told me that he once started counting them. After reaching 3,000 he gave up — and went fishing instead.

Sutherland, Caithness and Ross-shire offer wonderful game fishing amidst some of Scotland's most dramatic scenery. There is excellent salmon, sea-trout and wild brown trout fishing, the majority of which is readily available to visiting anglers. Scourie in North-West Sutherland, for instance, with more than 300 trout lochs to choose from, including such outstanding salmon and sea-trout systems as Loch Stack, a silver gem lying between the grey shoulder of Arkle and shapely cone of Ben Stack.

Outboard motors are not allowed on Stack and in times past seasoned, experienced gillies used to row their gentlemen over the most productive drifts.

One such gillie, towards the end of his career, carried out his duties more by instinct than by reason: he had always been short-sighted, but, nearing retirement, he could hardly see his hand in front of his face. Eventually, at the end of a long hard day on Loch Stack, he was persuaded to hang up his oars by two old friends. The last fish he had landed was a magnificent sea-trout weighing 6lb and, as he applied the priest, he was telling his companions about a similar fish, caught by his father in the dim and distant past: "A beautiful fish, gentlemen, just like this one is." "Willie," called his gentleman, "Willie, the other end." The gillie, blind as a bat, was bashing away at the fish's tail. So he agreed to call it a day. But I still have a map drawn by one of his colleagues, marking all the main sea-trout and salmon lies on Stack; worth its weight in gold, quite irreplaceable.

The best Scourie brown trout lochs require a fair degree of fitness to reach. They lie scattered amongst the hills and moorlands and skill using a compass and map is almost as important as skill using a fishing rod.

Even if you are familiar with the terrain, it is very easy to get lost, particularly if a sudden mist descends. One loch looks very much like any other and some are not even marked on the 1:50,000 map, so always be properly clad and prepared to cope with fickle weather conditions, before setting out.

One year, when my wife Ann and I were leading a party of friends into the hills, we decided to split up. I would take two out in the boat on Gorm Loch, Ann would bank fish the lochans with the others. Knowing my ability as a direction finder, Ann kindly left me the map and wandered off. After about twenty minutes, walking and fishing, she realised that she was hopelessly lost. Nor were her companions anywhere to be seen. Her faithful shadow, a Yorkshire terrier called Heathcliffe, was just as confused; and the time that we had arranged to meet for lunch was fast approaching. Turning her back on Ben Stack, Ann struck off in as straight a line as possible, eventually arriving at the main road, about three miles east of Scourie. She then walked back to our original starting point and retraced our morning route along the Gorm track, finally arriving for lunch only ten minutes late but having walked nearly nine miles. Relief all round.

However, given a reasonable state of preservation, you should come to no harm at Scourie; and most days will see you happily tramping anything up to six miles, fishing perhaps a dozen different waters along the way, with golden eagle, red deer and curlew for company. The best sort of fishing.

The only problem is knowing where to begin and a good place to start is at one of the best known fishing hotels in the north, Scourie Hotel, owned and managed by Ian Hay and his family for more than thirty years.

Scourie is a small village by the sea at the end of the road from Lairg to Laxford; a few houses, attractive caravan site, shop, post office, and not much else. The hotel stands on the site of the home of General Hugh Mackay (1640-92), who joined the English army in 1660, serving in France and Holland, eventually returning to England with William of Orange, in the Revolution of 1688.

Mackay had no love for the Jacobite cause and in spite of his defeat at the Battle of Killiecrankie, he was given the task of subduing the Highlands, where he built the fort at the head of Loch Linnhe which became known as Fort William. Mackay died, personally leading his troops into the thickest of the fight at the Battle of Steenkirk in July 1692.

Ian Hay leads his troops of visiting anglers with similar verve and spirit, and fishing at Scourie is organised with almost military precision; using a system that is exclusive to the hotel and which is being increasingly emulated by other Scottish fishing establishments. I have fished all over Scotland but the first place that I came across this system, which is used to distribute available fishing fairly amongst guests, was at Scourie, and it works very well indeed.

The system is centred round a board master, who is generally one of the senior guests present. Might sound a bit complicated, but if we take it slowly, all will be revealed, and you will see that by using this method, every guest has an equal share of fishing opportunities.

When you arrive at the hotel your name goes to the bottom of a list of other fishing guests' names, displayed on a blackboard. At the end of each day's fishing, the top name goes to the bottom, and your name automatically progresses up the list, eventually reaching the top.

After dinner, the person at the top of the list is offered first choice of all the hotel water and selects where he wants to fish the following day. Wherever he wants to go. The remainder of the fishing is then offered by the board master to each guest in turn, according to his position on the board, second top, third top, and so on.

The board master performs this service on a voluntary basis and the prerequisite of being board master is knowing the fishing thoroughly; because he has to tell new guests where to go, how to get there, which path to take, which bog to avoid, where not to fall in — so he really must know what he is talking about.

Board masters are guests with years of experience of Scourie fishings, and my favourite is a wonderful gentleman called Stanley Tuer; a man of advancing years, but fleet of foot, who has exhausted me on many a long hill walk. He has been an angler all his life, in spite of the inconvenience of having to make his living as a school master. However, even this chore was quickly organised to accommodate regular visits to his beloved Scourie.

Starting his career in the Midlands, over the years Stan worked up both the educational establishment and the country, aiming ever nearer Scotland; until finally arriving at Carlisle, where he held his last post. Come holiday time, Stanley closed the school and was off north quicker than you could say algebra.

When Stan retired, he settled in Dornoch, the market town of Sutherland, close to excellent facilities, shopping and medical services; but of far greater importance, within an easy hour's drive of Scourie.

Stanley has been going to Scourie for more than twenty years and knows every single blade of grass and stone, by name; he can take you to a loch and point out precisely where you will catch fish and where you won't, to the inch, and Stanley is never wrong. In some places he will say: "Well, we won't bother fishing here, we will walk on to the next loch", where you invariably catch a fish or two. On one such occasion, I had walked past a tiny lochan. Stan called me back: "Worth a cast, Bruce. See if you can get your fly out towards the middle. If you do, you might just hook a beauty." I did, and it was; a fine trout weighing just over 2lb.

This is the sort of individual who is eventually invited to become a board master and the system engenders a wonderful sense of anticipation, as you progress up the board towards the prime positions; when you are going to have your special day, on your favourite loch. In spite of ghosts.

Sorry, I forgot to mention the ghosts. Not the "go bump in the night" kind, but the spirits of departed guests. You see, if three guests suddenly leave, after their fishing holiday, when you are at position four on the board, your name is catapulted to top position — missing out on second- and third-best positions, which is bad news given the quality of all the fishing available. Hence the ghosts. Although the guest may no longer be there — gone home — his name remains on the board so that the orderly upward progression might continue, thus ensuring fair distribution of fishing.

Consequently, the board master is a person of great status in the hotel and his ancient function is highly revered. For instance, in days gone by, when angling guests used to sit round one table, the board master was known as "chief fork". He was always served first. When the hotel only had one toilet, it was the board master's privilege to have first use every morning. When there was only one bathroom, at the end of the day's fishing, the board master always had the right of the first, peaty splash.

These traditions are remembered and respected, although rooms in the hotel now all have private bathrooms. Nothing Spartan about present-day Scourie; but the board master still sits alone at meal-times, at a small table at the side of the dining-room, divorced from the influence of other guests. He even has his own chair in the lounge, close to the fire, and it is decorated with a beautifully embroidered head cloth, displaying his auspicious title, the handsome work of one of Scourie's regular lady guests.

As can be imagined, in a place with such grand fishing traditions, people who go there regularly often become associated with particular lochs; and that is very much part of the charm of fishing at Scourie. For example, certain lochs are named after guests, and the most recent naming was Yeoman's Loch; a tiny, Y-shaped lochan at the end of a long, hard trek.

Roger Yeoman was passing one morning, and just happened to notice movement under the surface. He chanced a few casts and by the end of the season he had taken more than a dozen good trout. So the board master and the proprietor, "sitting in solemn conclave", decreed that, "henceforth and forevermore, the loch shall be known as Yeoman's Loch". And it is.

In days when guests used to go out on the hill with gillies if they were fishing a large loch, and caught undersized trout, they didn't put these small fish back; instead, they put them in a bucket, taken along for the purpose, and carefully carried the little fish to an adjacent lochan. The trout were then released, secretly, and left to grow to great size.

Guests do the same today and most Scourie regulars have their own, small, personal, private larders. The trick is to stumble on one of these Aladdin's caves of fishing delight — and wreak havoc. That is why, when fishing at Scourie, you have to be very cautious, no matter where you cast; it might well be just another small trout heading for the breakfast frying pan, but there again, it could be a monster, heading straight for the glass case.

Another Scourie loch which has a delightful story does not really lie within the boundary of the hotel fishings. Nearly, but not quite; and when guests come back after a hard day in the hills, displaying half a dozen beautiful fish, and are asked where they caught them, they might reply "Shhhh", rather than admit malpractice. So the loch is known as the Hush Loch.

Even in the best regulated circles, at times people are tempted. General Hugh Mackay, a soldier's soldier if ever there was one, would understand; as indeed, I'm sure, a more modern general would have, a local landowner who had a very good, private trout loch near Scourie.

When news was brought to the hotel that the general had, "passed on to that great trout loch in the sky", people were genuinely saddened because the general had been a much-respected member of the community. However, on the morning of his funeral, two senior guests, reading their papers after breakfast, raised quizzical eyebrows: "Well, the General will not be needing his loch this morning," said the one to the other. Newspapers were quietly folded and they headed for the hills. But the old soldier had the last laugh. In spite of their best efforts, the miscreants returned fishless.

Another retired military gentleman, a colonel, was a regular visitor to Scourie. He arrived one year with his third wife, and the ashes of his late-lamented second wife tucked away in the boot of his car. Ian Hay told me the lady's last wish had been that the Colonel should scatter her ashes in the headwaters of the River Laxford: "But, you see, his new young wife was not the sort of lady to enjoy much walking and the poor Colonel just didn't know how he was going to get the job done. So I arranged for one of the estate stalkers to take the remains up the river, when the Colonel and his lady were out for the day."

Towards evening, Ian thought that he had better make certain that everything was in order, before the Colonel returned, and telephoned his friend: "Now Ian, everything is just as fine as it should be; you can tell the Colonel that his good lady will be well out to sea by now."

My wife Ann and I first visited Scourie in 1974, along with our two children, Blair and Lewis-Ann. We had a splendid holiday, walking and fishing, full of memorable moments: surprising a pair of red-throated divers on a lochan along the Gorm Track; a raven,

41

at the Black Rock; and a brief glimpse of Grandad, Scourie's largest resident trout.

Some of the Scourie trout, released into small lochs as tiny fish, have grown to enormous size and are known affectionately by name: Ethel, stocked by Stan Tuer when she was a modest girl of five inches, now estimated to weigh at least 5lb; Arthur, estimated to weigh 6lb. He lives in a loch on Mrs Little's beat.

But Grandad is enormous. One guest once saw Grandad move out of his lair by a lone rowan. Grandad had never been hooked, but on this occasion, he grabbed a Blue Zulu, went off like a rocket and soon broke the cast; that was about ten years ago: the first and last time anyone came near to catching him.

Knowing where to fish is the real key to success at Scourie and one year Stan took Ann and me to one of his favourite lochs, close to Ben Stack. We stopped some distance from the bank and as we put up our rods, Stan explained the plan: "Bruce, do you see that headland, over there, to the right? Well, that is known as Pennel Point. The first angler each season to stand there and cast out a Black Pennel, about ten yards, always catches a trout of 1lb." I listened intently. "Are you sure, Stan?" I asked. "Just do it," came the peremptory reply.

Ann, made of sterner stuff than I, refused all invitations to have the first cast and eventually, crouching below the skyline, I reached the appointed place. My Black Pennel whisked through the air and settled delicately on the surface. I held my breath and waited for that savage tug; and waited, and waited, and waited. I cast again. And waited, and waited. Not a dimple disturbed the surface. "That's funny," said Stan, shaking his head in disbelief. "That's never happened before. Are you sure you have a Black Pennel on?"

Nothing daunted, we fished round the loch and caught our fair share, but nothing from the fabled Pennel Point. Perhaps there was a chink in the Tuer armour?

The following year, my son Blair and his wife Barbara joined us. As we approached the loch, in order to impress Blair with my vast knowledge, I repeated Stan's tale about Pennel Point, being careful not to mention who had given me such valuable information.

Blair crept down to the bank whilst I rehearsed various reasons to explain why he had not caught the trout: lack of experience, bad casting technique. Poor Blair would then feel guilty, having missed a fish that Father would most certainly have landed.

The moment Blair's flies touched the water, there was a mighty swirl. The reel began to screech in protest as a fine trout tore off into the distance, leaping spectacularly along the way. After a great struggle Blair landed the fish and brought it over to where I was standing, mouth agape. "Thanks, Dad, that was jolly sporting of you to let me have first cast. Look, it must be nearer 2lb than 1lb. Do you know any other points like that round here?" I grimaced weakly. "Why are you laughing, Ann?" Blair asked his mother. All was revealed, including my discomfort.

But size and numbers of fish caught are of little importance at Scourie. This is the place for the complete angler; for the fisherman who loves the wild, distant places of Scotland. During my last visit, on a warm spring day, I climbed high into the remote vastness of Foinaven and Arkle, to a tiny blue speck of water, probably unfished for decades. As my flies touched the surface, two trout, each weighing about 10oz, greedily grabbed; and each successive cast brought two more. The fish were in perfect condition, tinged green from their mountainous surroundings and I kept two, for the record, releasing the others to fight another day.

Time passes quickly in Sutherland, almost unnoticed in the hills; and as long shadows gathered in secret corries, I took down my rod and walked home, full of wonderful memories to warm cold winter nights. Enduring dreams of Scourie.

TOFTINGALL

IONCE mentioned to a local farmer that my grandfather had been born in the little fishing village of Staxigoe, to the north of Wick in Caithness, and he quickly warned me not to go about repeating the story, because of the supposedly dubious reputation the natives of Staxigoe have earned themselves down the ages. Which was probably just green cheese. Staxigoe used to be far more important than Wick; a busy fishing port, where Scandinavian timber was imported and the small harbour bustled with boats long before Wick gained pre-eminence as the most notable herring fishing station in Europe during the nineteenth century.

We moved to Caithness in 1975 for a number of reasons, not least of which was the family connection. But Caithness also offered everything we valued: remote, empty moorlands, magnificent, wave-lashed cliffs capped by lovely wild flowers, bird life in abundance, superb empty beaches and, for us, the greatest attraction of all, some of the finest brown trout fishing in Scotland.

Caithness, mainland Scotland's most northerly county, is quite unlike its wilder neighbour, Sutherland. Between the Royal Burgh of Wick, the administrative centre on the east coast, and Thurso to the north, lies a fertile plain, stocked with the fine North Country Cheviot sheep for which Caithness is famous, and neat, well-tended fields of oats and barley.

Beyond these fields, moorlands rise and fall in gentle folds, southwards to where dramatic Caithness mountains line the horizon: Scraben, Maiden Pap, Morvern, Ben Alisky and Beinn Glas Choire. Westwards, past the Ben Griams in Sutherland, out to the jagged peaks and pinnacles of Scotland's "Queen of Mountains", Ben Loyal, lies the Flow Country, a wilderness land of lochs and lochans, untouched by the hand of man for more than 5,000 years.

This area became our most precious place; where we took the children to teach them how to fish; to watch black, and red-throated divers, golden eagle, golden plover, greenshank and dunlin; where we could walk endless miles with only the sky and the wind for company. A special place.

Sadly, since 1979, and in spite of national and international protest, much of the land we loved has vanished forever beneath an ever-increasing canopy of foreign conifers. More than 100,000 acres have been drained, ploughed and planted, destroying a unique landscape, along with its dependent wildlife. Lochs which were once as clear as crystal are now coloured muddy brown. Silt, washed from deep forestry ploughing, smothers plants, endangering insect life and therefore fish survival also. There is evidence of damage to spawning grounds, caused by forestry flash-flooding; hills are scarred by new roads; locked gates and electrified fences bar the way across the moors.

All this has been done in the name of spurious progress: to create jobs in rural communities, provide employment. Upwards of £12m of tax-payers' money has been invested in these new forests and at present, in Caithness, forestry has provided only three full-time jobs for local people; at the cost of the greatest act of environmental vandalism perpetrated in Scotland this century.

If any of our political masters, the faceless bureaucrats, the time-serving, vote-chasing, career politicians who sanctioned this devastation, ever read these lines, then I curse them for their crass stupidity and their wanton rape of my native land. As for the so-called foresters who jumped on the tax-avoidance bandwagon and ruined our moorlands, then I hope their consciences trouble them to their dying day. They have been responsible for destroying one of earth's greatest treasures.

During the planting years, I have known personally most of the tree-farmers involved. Self-assured young men, imbued with forestry propaganda. Most have long since gone, leaving behind their legacy of sunless, blanket afforestation. Nor have they any legal commitment to managing the monstrous forests they created for their absentee landlords. The moment it becomes unprofitable to do so, there is no doubt in my mind that the tree-farmers will abandon these forests. In 1988, amidst a great burst of publicity, one forestry company announced plans for the future management and improvement of a river they owned. They sold the river less than two years later.

Forestry interests currently own more than forty Caithness and East Sutherland trout lochs. What will become of them? Will they too be sold to the highest bidder, regardless of the interests of local people?

Many of the lochs we used to fish are now affected by forestry: Meala, Sletill, Leir, Talaheel, Lochan nan Clach Geala, The Cross Lochs, Caol, Garbh, Skyline, Caise, Meadie, Cherigal, Gaineimh, Eileanach, Dubh nan Geodh and Toftingall.

If you value the quality of Caithness game fishing, and the beauty of Scotland's wild and lonely places, write to Scottish Secretary, Malcolm Rifkind, St Andrews House, Edinburgh, demanding that all further planting in the Flow Country be stopped, immediately, whilst there is still something left to be saved.

Toftingall, which lies a few miles south from the village of Watten, was one of the first Caithness lochs we fished. It covers an area of some 150 acres and is very shallow; indeed, prior to mass-afforestation, it was possible to wade from one side to the other, without danger, because the water was so clear.

Although surrounded by peat moorlands, Toftingall rests on a gravel base and has a pH of approximately 7.5. Consequently, it hosts an excellent wild brown trout population and fish are pink-fleshed and fighting fit, averaging 10oz in weight.

Toftingall is at the centre of Caithness and in times past was the meeting place for local clans, who gathered there prior to setting off south in search of revenge, plunder or just a jolly good fight. Even in recent years, Toftingall was a place of refuge for outlaws and bandits. Backless Hill, to the north of the loch, was the eighteenth-century lair of a Caithness "Robin Hood", said to have robbed the rich and given to the poor. Apparently, not everyone agreed, or perhaps did not get what they considered to be their fair share, for eventually the Backless baron was transported to Australia, no doubt to become another "Wild Colonial Boy".

We used to visit Toftingall frequently, not only to fish, but to delight in the wide variety of bird life that called the loch home. During winter months, hundreds of grey-lag geese roost on Toftingall. They come from the Arctic, to winter in Caithness, as do flights of wild whooper swans from Iceland.

One year, in June, we found a pair of swans still at Toftingall. They should have flown north in March, but perhaps they weren't paying attention when the others left, maybe deep in conversation or looking the other way. The graceful pair brightened many a summer evening.

The moorlands also used to be a larder for great raptors: hen harrier and short-eared owl, quartering the heather in endless search of prey. I once watched an osprey fishing in the loch. I had spent four hours catching nothing and he simply swooped down and lifted a trout of at least 2lb from under my nose. My only consolation was that, much to my astonishment, the bird dropped the fish. So I wasn't the only duffer around after all.

Another frequent visitor was the black-throated diver. Unlike their more common cousins, red-throated diver, these birds require larger expanses of water upon which to take off and land. A clear flight path; but they are invariably curious and often drift close to the boat. Making sure that you are fishing fairly.

In windy conditions, Toftingall becomes impossible to fish, because the bottom is churned up, clouding the water. A few days later, things settle back to normal and sport is generally excellent. An average day sent us safely home with at least a dozen nice trout weighing some 5lb, with the occasional larger fish of up to 3lb. Depending, of course, upon which fingers you crossed.

I always preferred bank fishing Toftingall and invariably had better results than from fishing from the boat. The only problem with bank fishing is providing a steady stream of waders, or rather non-waders. They never seem to last. Not like the old, stiff, black ones I used to have when I was a boy. These were indestructible and to this day I regret ever falling for the slick adverts for trendy green ones.

It is even worse with a family of six anglers. Costs a fortune. Nowadays, I tend to do without. I strip up, removing trousers and pulling on a pair of light-weight leggings, and just wade in. During the early months of the season I catch my breath a bit, but the body is wonderfully adaptable and I do manage to reach parts of the loch others never cover.

Jean, my youngest daughter, once decided to emulate my habit. I watched her pulling on leggings and splashing in. A few moments later, she came ashore and wandered over: "Dad, these leggings don't seem to work, water is still getting in," she complained.

On a hot summer day, Toftingall is a super place for a splash and my golden retriever, Breac, the gaelic name for trout, used to spend hours in the loch. Unlike my wife Ann's Yorkshire terrier, who hates water. In fact, we had to teach him to swim, and did so at Toftingall.

Instead of trying to walk, doggy paddle, Heathcliffe always tried to climb out of the water; hence, he generally ended up on his back, legs lashing away hopelessly, until disappearing under the surface. Sometimes, when he had been sitting near the side of the boat, an ill-considered back cast sent him flying into the water; and often it was a close run thing before I could get the landing net under his sodden frame.

The last time this happened I just managed to catch a glimpse of his two black eyes, going down for the third time, before I landed him. That decided me. I took him up to Toftingall, attached a long rope to his collar, waded out, placed him afloat and then hauled him ashore, head first. He eventually got the hang of it but to this day, keeps well clear of water.

In spite of recent forestry around Toftingall, fish are still there, but for how much longer remains to be seen. However, if you don't mind fishing in water the colour of Brown Windsor soup, you may have good sport. Access by car is easy now, down a forestry road, almost to the edge of the loch. There is a good boat and up to ten bank fishing permits are issued each day.

Happily, the principal Caithness lochs have not been affected by the tree planters, and visiting anglers will find splendid sport on outstanding waters such as Watten, St John's and Heilen, all readily available at modest cost. The pH of these excellent lochs is in the order of 7.9 and trout are of exceptional quality.

My favourite Caithness loch is Heilen, near Castletown; an expert's loch if ever there was one. I can count the number of trout that I have taken from this lovely loch on the fingers of one hand and blank days are the rule, but I keep going back for more.

Heilen is very shallow and weedy. Indeed, after July there are very few weed-free areas and a good knowledge of the loch is required to find suitable areas to fish. The average weight of Heilen trout is in the order of 2lb 8oz and to take fish of lesser weight is a crime. In May 1987, a magnificent specimen of 7lb 8oz was caught and my best fish weighed 4lb 8oz.

Heilen trout are, in my opinion, some of the most beautiful wild brown trout in Scotland and they fight more furiously than you can ever imagine. In recent years, I have preferred launching my attack from the bank, rather than from the boat; and even in high winds, when most of the loch is churned up, clear patches of water may be found along the lee shore.

When angler friends visit me in Caithness, I always persuade them to fish Heilen, and invariably, suffer in consequence: "Bruce, you are quite mad. There isn't a single fish in this loch. I swear it." We sit all day, without seeing the smallest ripple and my credibility plummets.

One wild evening, when the wind was howling and rain lashing down, I took Peter Brewer, a Somerset bank manager up to the loch, much against his better judgment. "Look, couldn't we just go along to the pub and have a quiet drink and talk about fishing instead?" he pleaded. We assembled our rods in the shelter of the old boathouse on the south shore and I strode purposefully to the loch, almost as a matter of principal. I estimated that perhaps fifteen minutes' fishing would salve my honour, and not expecting to catch anything, I let the wind flag my flies out over the water.

The tail fly, a size 14 Silver Butcher grazed the surface and immediately the water erupted. A superb trout hooked itself firmly and during a breathtaking few minutes gave a spectacular display and a wonderful fight. I landed the fish, which weighed 3lb, and turned to show it to Peter.

His place by the boathouse was empty. Twenty yards away, through the storm, I glimpsed his figure, furiously lashing away as though his last fishing moment had come. I wandered down. "I think that you are right, Peter, this is madness. Shall we head for the pub?" But answer came there none.

To the north of Heilen is Loch St John's, one of the best-known trout lochs in Scotland, famous for the size and quality of its trout; and also famous for its ability to cure depression.

Tradition has it that in times past people brought their sick and weary to the shores of the loch, certain of its curative properties. The treatment involved walking three times round the shore and then departing, without looking back. If these rules were followed, then all cares and troubles vanished; as we say in Scotland, like snow off a dyke.

True or false, it is hard to be depressed at Loch St John's, particularly if you are a trout fisherman. The loch has some splendid fish and, in late June and early July, a wonderful mayfly hatch. Anglers come from all over Britain to fish St John's and rarely depart unhappily.

The loch is managed by an excellent group of local anglers who, some years ago, formed the Loch St John's Angling Improvement Association. Given constant fishing pressure, measures were needed to maintain stocks of fish; and the association established a hatchery where trout of native stock are carefully reared to fingerling stage and then released into the loch. This has resulted in a temporary drop in the average weight of fish, as the trout population increases, and St John's trout now average approximately 10oz. Nevertheless, each season fish of much greater size are caught and the monsters that made St John's famous are still there, waiting for your well-presented cast.

Watten is the largest Caithness loch, three-and-a-half miles long by up to three-quarters of a mile wide, and is best fished from the boat. With a trout-rod. I mention this only because it is possible, in the rush to get afloat, to forget that most essential piece of equipment. I know, I have done so.

A few years back, my mother was staying with us; a lady of advancing years but still a very keen angler. The only problem is organising her into the boat. I am invariably treated like an irresponsible five-year-old, not to be trusted, and at times "things" become rather heated.

On this particular occasion, the first fight was about getting Mother into suitable wet-weather gear. After a great struggle, I frog-marched her into oilskins and over-trousers, fitted the outboard and set off up the loch, perspiring.

I turned the boat into the first drift and bent down to pick up the rods. No rods. I looked under the seats. No rods. Without a word, I restarted the motor and headed back to the mooring bay, half a mile distant, encouraged by a running commentary: "Why are we going in? We haven't started fishing yet. Have you forgotten your cigarettes? That's it, isn't it. How many times have I told you that you should give up smoking but you never listen to what I say. You have always been the same, never do what you were . . ." I moored the boat, got out, collected the rods from the shore, and turned back up the loch. This time, I was spared the monologue. Mother couldn't speak for laughing.

The day ended with three fish, one of which was a very nice trout weighing 1lb 8oz. Mrs Sandison senior was sitting in the stern, complaining about the lack of rising fish, and the useless flies that I had mounted on her cast, when the trout grabbed. Amidst the usual panic that surrounds such occasions, I tried to keep calm and asked Mother to hand me the landing net. As she leaned forward to do so, before our very eyes the trout leapt from the water, about three feet in the air, did a neat twist and landed at my feet in the bottom of the boat.

For once, Mother was almost speechless. All she could mutter was, "Bruce, if I hadn't seen it with my own eyes, I would never have believed it."

MORTON

I N THE twelfth century, Nithsdale was ruled by Dunegal, a Scottish chieftain of Irish descent. Then Clan Douglas established their dynasty, and until the present day, the Douglas family, in their various departments, have played a major part in shaping Scotland's story.

Morton Castle, near Thornhill, was a Douglas stronghold of considerable importance. The first Lord Douglas died in captivity in 1298, a prisoner of Edward I, "Hammer of the Scots", and his son, Sir James, the "Black Douglas", was the principal lieutenant and a staunch friend of Robert Bruce during the Scottish Wars of Independence.

After the Battle of Neville's Cross, in October 1346, King David II and Sir William Douglas, "Knight of Liddesdale", were captured along with sundry other Scottish nobles. Edward III believed that he had broken Scotland's will to resist English domination. Later events were to prove how wrong he was, but in the meantime, William Douglas entered into protracted, frequently downright treacherous, negotiations to secure his release; including agreeing to allow Edward's armies unhindered passage through Liddesdale. King David, for his part, offered to dismantle Morton Castle.

William Douglas did not enjoy the fruits of his dubious labours long. In 1353 he was murdered by his godson, also William Douglas, in Ettrick Forest, and the new Lord Douglas established the enduring power of the family, which, in time, rivalled the very crown itself.

Today, the ancient name of Douglas is still well represented in Scottish affrays by the Dukes of Hamilton and Buccleuch, Earls of Home and Morton, Marquess of Queensberry, and Lord Torphichen.

The Douglas castle of Morton stands on a promontory, protected on three sides by a small loch. To the south-west, a deep moat, spanned by a drawbridge, completed defences. The present dramatic ruin probably dates from the sixteenth century, although it is believed that Dunegal had his manor house on the site in the twelfth century.

Two towers still exist, ten feet thick at their base, linked by an outward wall, ninety-six feet in length and thirty-six feet high. A groove in the gateway of the north-east tower marks the position of the portcullis; and although the northern part of the castle has long since disappeared, the original floor plan is easily discernible from the remaining foundations.

Kitchen and diningroom were massive, eighty-eight feet long by thirty feet wide, with a space for a huge fireplace at the east end. At the beginning of the last century, when repairs were being carried out to embankment walls enclosing the loch, a Pictish canoe hewn from a single, solid piece of wood was dug from exposed silt. No doubt the loch provided fish for the table as well as water for cooking and drinking.

The loch also seems to have been used as a dumping place for unwanted kitchen utensils. Soon after the canoe was dug up, a small copper kettle was discovered, and in 1728 a copper tea-pot stroup was found, still in excellent condition.

The castle was occupied until fairly recent times. The late Mrs Clerk-Douglas of Holmill relates that her great-grandfather was the last inhabitant, with the exception of an old woman, a servant of the family. She had lived so long within its walls that, when the great-grandfather of Miss Douglas found it necessary to abandon the castle from its ruinous state, she refused to do so and continued to find shelter there till her death, towards the beginning of the last century.

Morton Castle Loch still provides trout for the table and is an excellent fishery, owned and managed by Buccleuch Estates. The loch covers an area of eight acres and is stocked with brown, rainbow, and Canadian brook trout. A good boat is provided, rather than a pre-historic canoe, and visitors' use of a comfortable boathouse for shelter on wild days. Brown trout average 12oz, rainbow trout 1lb 3oz and brook trout 1lb 5oz. Morton is an attractive fishery, peaceful and serene, guarded by the red sandstone towers of the old castle on the hill. The estate also offer fishing on a smaller water, Starburn Loch, a mile south from Drumlanrig Castle.

Drumlanrig is a magnificent, pink castle, built between 1679 and 1689, by the first Earl of Queensberry, who spent only one night under its roof. Drumlanrig Castle and grounds are open to the public and contain something to interest every member of the family: Louis XIV furniture, paintings by Rembrandt and Holbein, woodland adventure play areas, picnic sites, nature trails, afternoon teas and gift shop.

Starburn Loch lies to the north of Tibbers Wood, where the ruins of another Douglas stronghold may be found; Tibbers Castle, destroyed by King Robert I in 1311, to deny possession of the fortified tower to the English.

The possession of salmon has also caused considerable acrimony between the two nations in times past, and the most infamous incident was the fish garth the English built across the River Esk, traditional boundary of England and Scotland, some time before 1474. This salmon trap denied upstream communities fish, then, as now, an important source of food. The English claimed that, "such right belonged to the King of England and his subjects by law and custom". The Scots disagreed and pulled the fish garth down.

By 1485, the English had rebuilt the Esk fish trap, but again it was quickly destroyed by the Scots. Various attempts were made to find a solution, in 1487, 1488, 1490 and 1491. To no avail. As soon as the English rebuilt the trap, the Scots pulled it down.

By 1513, the dispute had grown to such proportions that, before the Battle of Flodden, when James IV challenged the Earl of Surrey to single-handed combat to decide their two nations' grievances, the rewards to the victor were to include the return of the town of Berwick to Scotland, and the removal of the Esk fish garth. The fight did not take place, Surrey claiming that he was too lowly born to fight with a king; and the fish garth remained.

Claim followed counter-claim until 1543 when, under circumstances not recorded, some measure of agreement seems to have been reached.

However, the dispute over the Esk fish trap exploded again 300 years later, and almost resulted in civil war between Scotland and England. Sir James Graham of Netherby Hall rebuilt the trap and the Scots were so enraged that they gathered a small army of local people and set out to tear it down. Graham responded by collecting an army of his own, including a detachment of regular soldiers from the garrison at Carlisle. Fortunately, reason prevailed and Sir James agreed to open a gap in the garth, to allow fish upstream, and there the matter ended.

The border line between England and Scotland, the West Marches, along the line of the River Esk and its tributary, the Liddle, was recognised by all, at least up until about the end of the fifteenth century. Thereafter things became very confused, particularly with regard to the area known as the "Debatable Land", which both countries claimed.

For several hundred years, the "Debatable Land" was largely uninhabited and to keep it that way, in 1551, a proclamation was issued jointly by the two nations, to the effect that: "All Englishmen and Scottishmen after this proclamation is made are, and shall be, free to rob, burn, spoil, slay, murder and destroy, all and every such person or persons, their bodies, buildings, goods and cattle as do remain or shall inhabit upon any part of the said debatable land. Without any redress to be made for the same."

Settling the dispute took many years and several surveys, carried out by Bowes in 1542, 1550 and 1580; and Johnson and Goodwin in 1604 produced: "A survey of the Debatable and Border Lands adjoining the Realm of Scotland and belonging to the Crown of England, taken in 1604."

More immediate disputes, of which there were many, were sometimes settled at the Lochmaben Stone, one mile west from the mouth of the River Sark. The Lords of the West Marches and their Commissioners from both sides of the border, wherever that was thought to be at the time, met there to resolve complaints and grievances.

One huge stone still stands at Lochmaben: seven feet-ten inches high, weighing about ten tons. It used to form part of a larger circle, probably Neolithic, and up until fairly recent times, four upright stones remained. A local farmer, annoyed because they spoilt the symmetry of his field, and were awkward to plough round, decided to have them removed; but because of their weight, rather than attempting to drag them away, he ordered his workers to dig them underground. The proprietor, Lord Mansfield, arrived on the scene in time to save the last stone.

South-west Scotland has suffered much in recent years at the hands of more persistent "improvers": tree-farmers. Hundreds of thousands of acres have been ploughed and planted, principally at the tax-payers' expense, and primarily for the benefit of wealthy, absentee landlords. The old landscape has been radically altered, severely damaging wildlife and the environment.

These new forests have also had a disastrous effect on the quality of loch fishing. The rock structure of much of this area is granite and naturally acidic. Conifers, coupled with increasing atmospheric pollution, have greatly increased the acidity of many lochs and streams, seriously reducing their ability to sustain a healthy fish population.

Recently, and at vast expense, Loch Ken has been revitalised and restocked, because it had become fishless; and there is evidence that many other lochs, surrounded by conifer plantations, will need similar treatment to save them from ruin in the foreseeable future.

We first fished the South-west in the early 1960s when Ann and I paid a visit to Carsfad Reservoir, near New Galloway. In spite of being a reservoir, Carsfad provided excellent sport and we had great fun; as long as I steered well clear of the dam. Ann does not like dams.

Loch Doon, to the north, is much more attractive, to my mind, still retaining a wild, untamed atmosphere. Few salmon are encountered in Loch Doon these days, but brown trout abound and some huge fish have been caught in recent years.

Burns was also mightily attracted to Loch Doon and immortalized it in his song "Ye Banks and Braes o' Bonnie Doon", , written for Johnson's *Museum* in 1790. There is an even older version of the song, describing the fate of a young lady who died of a broken heart after being jilted by her lover.

Loch Doon was jilted during the First World War; there were plans to build an important sea-plane base there, but after the expenditure of some £500,000, the ill-conceived scheme was abandoned.

The loch contained five small islands, upon one of which stood Balliol's Castle, a ruined tower. The castle changed hands many times during the Scottish Wars of Independence and remained a thorn in the crown until James V sacked it in the sixteenth century; but before the level of the loch was raised in the 1930s, Balliol Castle was dismantled, ferried ashore, and rebuilt, stone by stone, on the north bank.

The River Doon flows out of Loch Doon through the narrow, deep gorge of Ness Glen, paralleling the twisting road that leads from Dalmellington out to the loch, bounded by wide, sweeping, desolate moorlands.

Dalmellington, when I knew it, was very much a traditional Ayrshire mining village, with friendly people, much given to laughter and fun. Particularly in the local pub. My problem in Dalmellington was not so much getting a drink, but in actually devising a means of drinking it. The roof of the pub was so low that I could not stand upright. I am six-foot four, and, in order to sink a pint, I had to sit down first. If all the seats were taken, then my only options were either to go outside, or kneel, as though in prayer. Which was good for the soul, but bad for knees and dignity.

The River Doon flows north-west from Dalmellington, past Patna and Dalrymple, under the Auld Brig o' Doon at Alloway, where Tam o' Shanter escaped from pursuing witches in Burns's magnificent poem:

> Now do thy speedy utmost, Meg,
> And win the key-stane of the brig;
> There, at them thou thy tail may toss,
> A running stream they dare na cross.

Robert Burns, regarded as one of the world's greatest and best-loved poets, was born at Alloway on 25 January 1759. The spark of poetry was kindled in him by an elderly woman who lived with the family and was full of tales of witches and warlocks.

In 1786, he published his first book, *Poems Chiefly in the Scottish Dialect*, now known as the *Kilmarnock Edition*; but in spite of this volume's modest success, and Burns's rapturous reception in

Edinburgh, most of the poet's life was spent in unrewarding toil as a farmer, and, latterly, as an Exciseman. And amongst the lassies. When Burns died, on 21 July 1796, his wife, loyal, long-suffering Jean Armour, could not attend her husband's funeral; she was busy giving birth to their last child. Burns had fourteen known children, half of them born out of wedlock.

Four of these infants are buried in Mauchline churchyard, where Burns and Jean lived in a house in Castle Street, now a museum. The slanderous epitaph Burns wrote for John Brown of Mauchline could have applied equally as well to the poet himself:

> Lament him, Mauchline husbands a,
> He aften did assist ye,
> Tho' ye had bidden years awa
> Your wives wad ne'er hae miss't ye.
>
> Ye Mauchline bairns, as by ye pass
> To school in bands thegither,
> O tread but lightly on the grass,
> Perhaps he was your father.

Across the road from the churchyard is Poosie Nansie's pub, the setting for Burns's poem "The Jolly Beggars", and is as welcoming today as it was in the time of Scotia's bard. In the bar is a superb chalk drawing of the drinking scene from "Tam o' Shanter", complete with Tam, and Soutar Johnnie "at his elbow".

Burns's poetry and songs have played an important part in my life from the earliest years, not only because of their simple beauty, but also because of their directness, honesty, and wry, lop-sided, humour; the appreciation of which stood me in good stead the last time I was in Mauchline.

A Glasgow friend, Tony Sykes, a great fisherman, at least he kept telling everyone he was, persuaded me against my better judgment to join him for a day's salmon fishing on the River Ayr at Mauchline.

I had never caught a salmon. Over the years I had hooked and lost many, and finally decided that there were far better ways of spending my time than in pursuit of these fractious, unpredictable, unco-operative brutes. Such as brown trout fishing, which remains my greatest angling pleasure.

But West of Scotland people are like that. The bigger the fish the better, and it would have been churlish to say no. It was April, and after a warmer in Poosie Nansie's, another West of Scotland custom, we thrashed away on the Ayr, casting amongst chunks of ice floating down the river; frozen stiff, getting colder and colder as the grey day grew older and older.

Eventually, I realized the exercise was a complete waste of time. We hadn't seen a fish, let alone hooked one. My fingers were numb and my whole body ached. "Tony," I called, "I have had enough. You will find me in Poosie Nansie's, by the fire. And if I had any sense I would never have left there in the first place."

By this time it was snowing hard. I struggled, Titus Oates-like, up the track to the road, leaving Sykes, glimpsed briefly through the white flakes, casting as a man possessed. Fishing should be fun, I thought, not a test of endurance.

I settled happily before the blazing fire, musing upon the stupidity of salmon fishing and certain of my friends. With my first dram halfway to my lips, the door burst open and in Sykes marched, snow-white from head to toe. "Well, thank goodness for that!" I exclaimed. "You are not completely daft after all."

Sykes smiled wickedly. From behind his back he produced a beautiful salmon, sea-liced and weighing about 8lb. "That's the trouble with you fair-weather Edinburgh anglers. No staying power. If you want to catch salmon, Bruce, you must be prepared to suffer a little discomfort. Still, you had your chance. Buy me a dram and I will tell you all about it."

I did and he did. For the next hour. In fact for years. Every time salmon fishing was mentioned, the old story about soft, city fishermen was trotted out, much to my discomfiture.

Five years later Sykes turned the knife even further: "You remember that salmon I caught on the Ayr in 1962? The day you retired hurt?" I gritted my teeth and nodded, refusing to be drawn. "Well, do you want to know how I really caught it?" Trapped in a nightmare of indecision, I reluctantly agreed and prepared myself for the worst.

Sykes had been as cold and miserable as me, hoping against hope that I would surrender first. As soon as I disappeared up the path, Poosie Nansie-wards, he promised himself one more cast followed by a quick canter to the bar. Having done so, Sykes took down his rod and prepared to make a dash for it, when through the storm he noticed two small boys. They were carrying a magnificent salmon. Within minutes, Sykes had struck a bargain, never stopping for a moment to ask where or how the fish had been caught.

But I had been caught, well and truly, and had paid the price, time and time again. Even worse. Telling the whole truth about the Ayr salmon, rather than letting me off the hook, only improved the tale. Which Sykes still tells, with relish, every time we meet.

ST ABBS

ODERN buses are not the same. They lack their predecessors' atmosphere. Old buses were much better. Travelling on them was always an adventure. Our first post-war holiday in 1947 was by bus, from St Andrew Square, Edinburgh. Destination: the tiny fishing village of St Abbs on the Berwickshire coast, seven miles north from Berwick-upon-Tweed.

I took with me, against my parents' will, a treasured possession: a plank of wood. To help me practise swimming quietly. It was essential. No other plank would do. In order to avoid a major rebellion, Father eventually gave in and lugged my piece of wood all the way to Berwickshire.

We stayed in a cottage on the cliffs, overlooking the harbour, and within moments of arrival, my brother Ian and I were at the end of the pier, fishing. Tackle consisted of a wooden frame around which was wrapped light, brown fishing-line, needle-sharp steel hooks, lead "sinkers" and a can of worms. Paradise.

The water in the harbour was extraordinarily clear. We could see fish, far below, nibbling our bait; and one morning I caught a tiny, incredibly beautiful, angle-shaped fish. I put it back, convinced that I had broken some serious law, hoping no one had noticed.

The only other thing I remember catching was my right thumb. With a hook. In order to get the bait out as far as possible, the lead weight was swung round and round, ever faster, and then released. The line must have tangled, because the next thing I knew, or rather felt, was a searing pain in my thumb as the hook dug in. The accident cost me a visit to the local doctor, and Mother several consolatory ice creams.

Ian's moment of glory came a few days later. He hooked and landed an enormous conger eel, whilst fishing from one of the boats in the harbour. Exactly where we had been swimming that morning. I had never seen anything so fearsome and kept well back until he despatched the beast; which seemed to take hours, and several hours later we were still trying to untangle Ian's line.

Each morning we ran down to the harbour to watch the previous night's catch being landed. There were always crabs and lobster. Huge, blue-black, shining, nightmare lobster. The fishermen showed us how to hold them safely and we invariably went home with a few, to watch, shocked, as Mother plunged them, alive, into boiling water.

For years I used to think that Shakespeare's line, "and roasted crabs hiss in the bowl", was about sea-food, describing the sound of boiling water, and claws, scratching vainly against the side of a hot, bubbling pan.

Our cottage was at the end of a fisherman's row, brightly painted, and owned by Mr Jake Nisbet. Jake was a wonderful character, full of tales and stories about his whaling days in the South Atlantic. He had a marvellous collection of carved whales' teeth and Ian and I believed every word he said.

Jake had a small boat, with inboard engine, and he would take us all out fishing below the sheer red, ragged Berwickshire cliffs. I was always allowed, at some stage of the adventure, to steer the boat; clinging to the rudder handle in an agony of excitement.

Jake also had a share in a larger, sea-going vessel, which we used to visit in the harbour, examining enviously the neat bunks and tiny galley. When we were invited to spend a night at sea with Jake and his companions, we accepted instantly.

Departure from St Abbs was to be shortly after sunrise; spend the whole day and night at sea, return the following morning.

Ian and I spent most of the night before at the window, terrified we would be asleep when Jake called; but we must have slept, because we were awakened by the sound of stones rattling against the window. Jake was below, true to his promise, waiting.

Jake was one of those people to whom "things" happened. Always something exciting. Twenty years after that holiday I read in the *Scotsman* one morning that a St Abbs fisherman had hauled in his nets and landed a complete suit of sixteenth-century armour. I knew instantly who the fisherman would be. I was right. Jake Nesbit.

We met another marvellous character at St Abbs; a lady who shaped and made aware hundreds of young minds; Jessie P. Young, teacher at the Edinburgh Royal High School's Junior School at Jock's Lodge. Miss Young was Ian's teacher, not mine, but from time to time she used to read to our class; and I was always captivated by her stories.

Jessie Young was on holiday in St Abbs but, nevertheless, took Ian and me out for a day, visiting Eyemouth and exploring Berwick. We walked the town walls, whilst Jessie Young told us breathtaking stories of battered Berwick's stormy history.

Berwick was the principal trading city of Scotland in the thirteenth century; but when King Alexander III fell from his horse near Kinghorn in Fife, on 19 March 1286, Scotland, without an obvious heir to the throne, fell also: into a 300-year nightmare of almost continual conflict with England. Edward I was asked to resolve the disputed succession and used the opportunity to assume control of Scotland, its revenues and administration. He arrived at Berwick on 2 August 1291 to determine the Great Cause and eventually, in 1292, found in favour of John Balliol.

The disappointed competitors divided Scotland and, after a treaty was established with France in 1296, an ill-conceived Scottish army gathered at Caddonlea near Selkirk to invade England. They were ignominiously defeated by the Earl of Surrey at Dunbar on 27 April.

Berwick was the next casualty. Edward captured the town and massacred its inhabitants. From then until 1318, when King Robert Bruce recovered the town for Scotland, Berwick was occupied territory.

Robert Bruce, grandson of Lord Annandale, one of the original competitors, was installed as King of Scotland in 1306, and the crown was placed upon his head by the Countess of Buchan. Later that same year, the Countess, Bruce's Queen, his sister Christina, and daughter Marjorie, were captured by the English. Edward arranged a terrible fate for Lady Buchan: "Because she has not struck with the sword, she shall not die by it. But verily, for that lawless coronation that she made, she shall be most firmly enclosed in a dwelling of stone and iron, made like a crown, and at Berwick be hung up in the open air, that she may be given, in life and after death, for a gazing-stock and an everlasting scorn to those who pass by."

Berwick was attacked by the Scots in 1312, and regained in 1318; besieged by Edward II in 1319; taken by the English in 1333; burned by James Douglas in 1405; ceded to Scotland in 1461 and returned to England in 1482 — where it remains, wrongly in my opinion, to this day.

Jessie Young fired my imagination with her tales of warfare, politics and terror at Berwick, and fanned in my heart the first flames of a lifelong fascination with Scotland's history. A number of her pupils, in their later years, formed the "J. P. Young Club" as a mark of their respect for this remarkable lady.

There was a continual passage of soldiers and armies, tramping backwards and forwards through Berwickshire, with the ebb and flow of battle between England and Scotland. The most obvious evidence of this warfare was reflected in buildings, such as Coldingham Priory, one of the most rebuilt places of worship in the Borders, the ownership of which was hotly disputed for centuries.

Coldingham Priory was founded as long ago as 635 AD. Coldingham New Church, relatively speaking, was built in 1220, and burned to the ground in 1420; then that great knocker-about of buildings and castles, Cromwell, passed in the mid-seventeenth century and removed a wall, presumably to keep his troops in training.

When Charles II reintroduced legal mirth and jollity to the kingdom in 1660, the old church was refurbished again, and when I visited it recently I was fascinated by the character of the place and how beautifully it was maintained.

But it was locked. I had planned to have a word with my Maker before walking on, but I couldn't get in. And I think this is regrettable, and certainly at variance with my early days. When I was a boy, God was always at home. Country churches were never locked; you could wander in at any time. Perhaps Cromwell, when he passed, also found the door of Coldingham Priory locked and decided that he would get in anyway, even if it meant removing a whole wall in order to do so.

If you walk out from Coldingham, past the delightfully ivy-covered Anchor Inn — work first, thirst later — you eventually arrive at Coldingham Loch. This excellent water is surrounded by mature woodlands and the estate used to be owned by the brewing family of Usher. Now the estate is in the hands of Dr Douglas Wise and Coldingham Loch has been developed into a very attractive fishery. Only a few acres in extent, shallow, but with superb feeding for trout, the loch is well managed and carefully stocked with both brown and rainbow trout.

Coldingham Loch was the first fishery in Scotland to introduce rainbow trout. These fish are native to North America and in recent years have been widely used to stock artificial fisheries throughout Britain. If they survive long enough, they begin to recapture many of their wild characteristics, but all too often it is a question of "put" and immediately "take". However, given the right conditions, they fight furiously, and Coldingham fish have a fine reputation. Back in the late 1940s, early 1950s, I remember my fishing mentor, the late Tom Kelly, Edinburgh, describing these wonderful, strange fish which displayed all the colours of the rainbow when they were caught; and I could hardly wait to have a go.

But it is not only trout that I have caught at Coldingham. I remember once catching a sand-martin. On the back cast. There was a tremendous hatch of flies and I was concentrating, hard, expecting a fish to grab any moment. I cast back and suddenly found that I had hooked the bird, which had been feeding avidly, dipping and swooping over the water. The poor beast flew round and round above my head in considerable distress. I gently reeled in, got him to my hand and carefully removed the fly, which had gone through the thin beak membrane. It can't have been very pleasant for the sand-martin, but for me it was a magical moment; to possess, momentarily, such a beautiful, wild creature. The bird lay in my palm, thistle-down light, then fluttered to freedom.

Coldingham estate has a number of comfortable self-catering cottages, and the most attractive of these is an old boat house, on the east shore of the loch. The building has been refurbished, and access is either by boat, or across trackless fields; but there can be few more attractive places to spend a fishing holiday, right on the edge of one of the Borders' most productive lochs.

The rise of "put-and-take" fisheries has paralleled a great

explosion of interest in game fishing; and as more and more people discover the delights of angling, tackle manufacturers have been quick to cash in on this growing demand. Each year some new, miracle rod is produced, and for the beginner, choosing the right rod is becoming ever more complicated. Me, I stick to my old sticks; and I think that the new breed of carbon-fibre rods are characterless. Carbon, glass, boron, graphite, hexagon, all seem lifeless to me; and high-modulus, high-strength aerospace technology leaves me about as cold as deep-frozen Arctic char.

A proper fishing-rod is built of either greenheart, or cane. Materials that live and breath. Rods made from them become treasured possessions. Old friends. Part of the family. I could never fall in love with fibatube. It wouldn't seem natural.

My first salmon-rod was a thirteen-foot greenheart. With a spike in the butt. For sticking into the ground. To keep the rod upright, out of harm's way when not in use. Never see rod-spikes these days. Father was given the rod by friends at West Linton, near Edinburgh, and it must have been about fifty years old at least, when it came into my possession.

Our local library, Macdonald Road, Edinburgh, produced a book on fishing that became my firm favourite. Other boys poured over Biggles and Enid Blyton: I devoured *The Fisherman's Vade Mecum*. I read it, cover to cover, endlessly, and practised casting for hours in the back garden, on the lawn. At times, I could see Father watching from the window, shaking his head in disbelief. John Macgregor Sandison was a golfer. He found it hard to understand what all the fuss was about, what possible pleasure there could be in waving a stick about for hours, catching nothing.

My older brother, Ian, was more interested in rugby; Fergus, younger, in horses. So at weekends I went fishing alone. Mother would make me a packed lunch; Dad deliver me to the bus station at St Andrew Square, Edinburgh. An hour or so later, I was fishing on Lyne Water, a beautiful tributary of the River Tweed.

Well, sort of fishing. Most time was spent retrieving ill-considered casts from trees, hunting in long grass for flies, cracked off. Flies were too expensive to be discarded lightly. Wading dangerously mid-stream to release flies caught on underwater obstructions, I rarely caught anything else.

But you always remember the first time. That moment of truth. When all the dreams come true. For some, a sparkling salmon after their first cast. Others, a hard-fighting, sea-liced sea-trout. For me, it was a five-inch brown trout, caught after two seasons of near-demonic effort. The rod tip dipped. My heart stopped beating. The brass reel gave a tentative click. I thought I had missed the fish and cried out in pain. I hurriedly cast again. The small trout came flying past my head, firmly attached to the tail fly.

In an agony of excitement, I searched in the long grass bordering the river, following the line to where the fish lay, gasping. It was utterly lovely. A creature of absolute beauty. Carefully, I removed the hook; and then, cradling the trout between cupped hands in the water, I waited until it darted off into the depths.

That sort of experience binds boy and rod together, and I used my old greenheart happily for many years to come; but in time, the top section broke, then the middle section, and eventually, I had the rod redesigned. Shortened into a beautiful, two-piece, seven-foot-long trout-rod.

All our children learned to fish, using this wonderful rod. It was the perfect weight for little arms. Blair, on the South Tyne, near Bardon Mill in Northumberland; Lewis-Ann, on a Scourie hill loch, in Sutherland; Charles and Jean, on Lochs Watten and Toftingall in Caithness. Which is a hard enough life for any man, and my old friend has retired now. As I write, he nods down at me from the wall beside my desk; shining brass-reel in place, cast and flies still ready for action, waiting for the last trumpet to sound.

The principal Border fishery is of course the mighty River Tweed, and there are a number of excellent trout lochs, near Hawick, and scattered along the coastal plain and in the Lammermuir Hills. But if I was pressed to make a choice, apart from Coldingham Loch, I would have to admit that the Whiteadder River is my favourite Border stream, and I confess that I have a vested interest in Whiteadder.

My wife and I spent the first days of our married life at Abbey St Bathan's, on Whiteadder, when we stayed with a remarkable lady, Miss Gillon, in her gardener's cottage. Miss Gillon was a member of the Turnbull Clan; famous for their insignia of a bull's head. The crest was granted to them by King Robert I of Scotland, when one of the family turned away a charging bull, threatening the King's life. Miss Gillon was just as active as any of her ancestors might have been. When we arrived she greeted us kindly, her first honeymoon couple, showed us round the cottage, then excused herself, saying that she had 600 lettuces to plant out before tea.

The nearest pub, a matter of some importance to me, and shop, were in Duns, and one afternoon we travelled there to re-stock depleted supplies. After buying groceries, I suggested a drink, and we wandered into the local inn.

Scottish country pubs are strange places, even more so thirty years ago. Ann was dressed in casual clothes, wearing particularly attractive trousers; you would call them "jeans" today. Nothing bright, but nevertheless, trousers. The bar was busy when we entered, buzzing with agricultural talk, but the moment we appeared, there was total silence. Thirty suspicious faces stared at us, pint tankards half-way to their lips. The barman rushed round the counter and grabbed my arm urgently, muttering: "This way, Sir, this way please. Bring the lady through here." We had our drink in dank, solitary, splendour, in the empty, cold, lounge bar.

The week we spent at Abbey St Bathan's was one of the happiest weeks of our lives. Springtime. Daffodils and primrose fluttered and blushed from warm corners. The whole world seemed to ache for summer's coming. Fish splashed in small pools and the sweet scent of the river hurrying by charmed our days.

In the evening, before a roaring open fire, we read; and talked endlessly about the ones that got away, and the few that didn't. Trout for breakfast, trout for tea. Happy times.

RANNOCH

IGHTY years ago Joicey Munro was a keeper on Dunalister Estate, Kinloch Rannoch, Perthshire; a Gaelic speaker with unswerving loyalty to the memory of Bonnie Prince Charlie, Pretender to the throne of Britain.

To hear Joicey speak, it was as though he had just left the Prince's side, and that the 1745 Rebellion had ended the previous day. Each year, when shooting, stalking and fishing guests departed, estate employees were called to the great house to work in the armoury, which had one of the finest collections of antique weapons in Scotland: claymores, dirks, shields, spears and guns. Men would set to, cleaning and polishing, burnishing brass, copper and silver. A relaxed gathering, with the hard toil of the year ended; when keepers, gillies and stalkers told stories about their gentlemen and ladies; about stags lost and stags shot, of grouse and salmon.

But Joicey had no time for such pleasantries. The armoury fired his Jacobite imagination and within seconds of arrival, he was re-fighting the Battle of Prestonpans, marching to Derby, advising General George Murray on tactics and encouraging the troops; in his mind's eye, waiting hand and foot upon his hero, Prince Charles Edward Stewart.

Sooner, rather than later, and generally after a few stiff drams, Joicey would break into the Gaelic, roaring and shouting at the top of his voice: "Man to man it was in those days. None of your bliddy cowering in trenches then." Joicey would grab a claymore and whirl it round and round, clearing an immediate circle in the room with everybody keeping their heads well down: "Man to man."

One year, when Joicey was in full flood, a new keeper made the mistake of challenging him: "Joicey, you don't know what you are talking about. Half the Highlanders ran away at Culloden without striking a blow; and as for 'man to man' — if you didn't keep your bliddy head down in the trenches, you got it blown off in half a second."

Joicey stopped, claymore clutched, eyes blazing furiously, face red with rage: "I'll show you what I mean, you heathen," Joicey roared. "Come here while I teach you how we fought in those days."

The keeper leapt to his feet as Joicey flew at him, slashing with the shining sword. They danced round the table, dodging this way and that: "Calm down, Joicey, I was only joking." "Joking, damn you, stand still and fight like a man."

Everyone looked on silently, wondering if Joicey had finally gone completely mad, as the young keeper swerved and ducked, growing more frightened by the minute. Eventually, Joicey cornered him, and in desperation, the keeper threw himself out of the nearest open window; landing ten feet below, with a badly sprained arm and sore head. Joicey leered over in triumph: "That will show you. Now come and have a dram with me, you daft idiot."

Joicey's love of the "water of life" frequently got him into trouble with the Laird. When parties went out grouse shooting, whisky was always taken for the beaters, keepers and loaders. The gentlemen had their own. Now, there were some who didn't drink, not many, and some who wouldn't drink, and Joicey always benefited from them all. By noon, he could hardly stand, let alone tramp over the moor, and he stumbled about, muttering away in Gaelic, complaining about working for a bunch of foreigners who had usurped his rightful King.

But he was well liked, and his colleagues, rather than see him lose his job, would roll the old man into a hollow, covering him with heather to keep out the damp, and leave him sleeping soundly until the end of the day. Then, when the Laird wasn't looking, they would dig Joicey up and help him home.

On one such occasion, when the head keeper and a young man were leading Joicey to safety, Joicey turned to the youngster and inquired: "Have you the Gaelic, lad, have you the Gaelic?" The man replied no, but that as he had been born and brought up at Moor of Rannoch, he had every right to call himself Scot. "Ach, man," groaned Joicey. "You are like the wild cat, you are not in it," meaning that present-day wild cats have become so inter-bred with domestic cats, they are no longer pure: like Scots who have lost their native tongue.

Rannoch is a wild place, full of wild stories from turbulent times of Scottish history, and Joicey Munro left his mark. He is still fondly remembered, many years after his last fight and final journey; no doubt with Prince Charlie, over that last, great sea to the sky.

The road from Pitlochry, past Tummel and Rannoch, is the fabled "Road to the Isles", and in times past this was an important Scottish highway. A few miles west from Garry Bridge is Queen's View, a rocky, pine-clad promontory with stunning views westwards down Loch Tummel to graceful Schiehallion.

Most people imagine that Queen's View is named after "unamused" Victoria, Scotland's most famous royal tourist, but in fact the lady in question was Mary, Queen of Scots, who visited Tummel in 1564, three years after her return from France. Mary, being over six feet tall, probably had a better view of the scene than her more traditionally built, runt-like Scottish companions, and she was enchanted by what she saw.

Poor luckless Mary never stood a chance. Even today Scots tend to be wary of clever women; but in those days, to be young, female, tall, beautiful, witty, talented and intelligent — and a Queen — was like writing one's own death warrant. Mary's self-seeking dandy courtiers soon made sure she signed it.

Schiehallion, one of Scotland's best-loved Munros — mountains over 3,000 feet in height — dominates Tummel and Rannoch. The peak was marked by Ptolemy, Egyptian geographer and astronomer, on the first known map of the British Isles; and it was here, in 1774, that Nevil Maskelyne, Astronomer Royal, conducted his experiments to determine the mean density of planet earth.

Westwards from Schiehallion, at the very heart of Scotland, lies Rannoch Moor, a desolate wilderness, 1,000 feet above sea level;

and across the moor, from west to east, like a silver scar, are a series of lochs and rivers offering excellent game fishing; plenty of space for everyone and plenty of fine wild brown trout. The fish aren't large and you are unlikely to return home with one that you could pop straight into a glass case, although you might well do so; but they fight hard and give a good account of themselves.

Trout tend to be in the order of half to three-quarters of a pound in weight and are great fun to catch. There are larger fish, particularly in Loch Rannoch, and since the end of the nineteenth century there are records of huge trout being caught, fish of up to 22lb; most seasons Rannoch still produces the odd monster.

These large fish are called ferox, a distinct species of brown trout that make their living by eating their smaller brethren. I suppose every one has to earn their keep, and the way to catch them is by using the old, traditional Scottish fishing method of trolling.

The technique employed is to attach a small trout, or even herring, to a bare hook. This is sunk to a depth of anything up to forty feet, on a lead-core line, and towed behind a slowly moving boat, fingers crossed. Boring work, but if you want one for the glass case, this is the best way to go about achieving that aim. I prefer walking and stalking to sitting and looking. Which is probably why my glass case is still empty.

Another wonderful aspect of Rannoch is the Black Wood, remnant of the great, natural pine forests that used to cover almost two-thirds of Scotland. The Forestry Commission are making valiant efforts to re-create these old woodlands, and are trying to preserve the little that remains.

The forests were cleared over the years for a variety of reasons: because people were scared of wolves, which roamed the area well into the seventeenth century; to make sure travellers could see robbers, before robbers saw them; to provide timber for ship-building: trees were felled and floated downstream through Loch Tummel and the River Tay to Perth. In fact, timber felling grew to such proportions that a law was passed restricting it; anyone found guilty of contravening this law more than three times, could be hung. Justice was rough and ready during Scotland's Middle Ages, very much designed to protect and preserve the influence of those in power. Hasn't changed much, either, when I come to think about it.

But we Scots were a bloodthirsty race then, and of all the black deeds that blacken Scottish history, I believe that the hunting of the Rannoch Macgregors was probably one of the most horrendous.

A branch of the clan lived along the shores of Loch Tummel and Rannoch, out to Gaur Bridge on the edge of the moor. Probably no better than they should be, thieving and robbing at will, they were known as the "Children of the Mist"; Rannoch can be a misty place and the Macgregors would appear, take your goods and chattels, and anything else not nailed down, then disappear again, into the mists of Rannoch Moor where they could never be found.

Their lawlessness became so notorious that James VI proscribed the clan, which turned out to be very unpleasant indeed, and his edict described them as: "that wicked race of lawless luminaries, callit the Macgregor". So it was open day for Macgregor-hunting and they were pursued like animals.

A reward was offered for the head of every Macgregor delivered to the laird; families were encouraged to betray their own people with promises of pardon; women were branded on the forehead; children were sold as little better than slaves to Lowland and Irish cattle dealers. Even the use of the name "Macgregor" was proscribed.

My wife, Ann, and I have experienced the sense of the terror that these unfortunate people must have felt, because it still lingers to this day in some of the small corries and glens in the hills above Tummel and Rannoch.

A few years ago, we were walking in the mountains to the south of Loch Tummel, heading for a tiny water called Loch a'Chait, a hard tramp uphill from Lick. It was a hot morning, with the sun beating down relentlessly, and we found the going hard; seemingly ever upwards. Eventually, we arrived at a small, damp valley, peat and heather-filled, where insects hummed in the still air.

I was halfway across the floor of this valley when Ann came running past; when I say running, I mean as fast as she could stumble over the uneven ground, pack on her back, carrying her fishing-rod. Her face was white with fear and she kept saying, almost whispering: "Quick, quick, get out of here, get out of here. Something terrible has happened." Without pausing, she hurried on and although I called after her she didn't stop until she had reached the other side and scrambled up the rocky gully to the top.

When I caught up, Ann was still obviously very distressed and I asked what on earth was wrong. She calmed down, and told me that she had a sudden impression, walking across the little valley, of women and children in great danger; nothing else, but a terrible feeling that women and children were about to be harmed.

It was then that I decided to learn more about what had happened to the "Children of the Mist" by the shores of Loch Tummel, and during my research an amazing possibility dawned. Often, before the arrival of the hunters, somebody tipped off the clansmen that the authorities were on the way. The first thing the men did, upon receiving the news, and before fending for themselves, was to move their women and children to safety, generally into one of the secret corries in the hills. But sometimes these hiding places were found; and I think that Ann and I had stumbled into one of these hiding places, where the women and children had lain, trembling with fear, listening to the sound of their approaching persecutors.

After resting, we tramped on up the hill to Loch a'Chait, arriving tired, hot and weary. I stripped off, laid my clothes out to dry in the sun, and cooled myself in the loch; then, standing on a rock, I surveyed the magnificent view, sure that the effort involved in reaching the loch had been more than repaid by its utter peace and serenity.

Which is when I heard the car. A distant buzz, drawing ever nearer. Amazed, I climbed the nearest rise and looked southwards. Inching up a well-made track, came an old, battered, dusty, Austin Allegro. Beyond, I could see the outline of a vast quarry, clearly from whence the car had come.

The car parked about a hundred yards from the loch and two men, clad in town clothes, got out and ambled over: "Any luck?" they inquired. They put up spinning-rods, and clutching a can of worms each, set off round the bank, in spite of admitting that they had no authority to do so.

Once round the loch and they headed back for their car, muttering that we were wasting our time because there was not a single fish in the loch. We watched them go and then settled down to some serious fly fishing, ending the day with four nice fish weighing 3lb.

We walked back that evening, avoiding Ann's valley, and reported to Major Whitson, the owner of the loch. The Major had told us that he was plagued with poachers, particularly since the new road had been driven up the hill from the Aberfeldy side; and that he very much doubted if there were any fish left in Loch a'Chait. We left him two for his supper.

Illegal fishing is a blight on Scottish sport. Not only poaching salmon, which is a growth industry, but also stripping brown trout lochs, using any means, fair or foul. Gangs of so-called anglers arrive, mostly from Central Scotland or the North of England, and their sole aim is to kill as many fish as possible.

Sadly, the law relating to brown trout fishing in Scotland is an ass, and few fisheries have any meaningful, legal protection from the attentions of such gangs of "fishmongers". In 1976, a new act was passed. The Freshwater Fisheries (Scotland) Act, allowing the setting up of a Protection Order for catchment areas; and several of these new orders are now in force, including one covering the Garry and Tummel Catchment Area. Just in time to preserve the high quality of sport and curtail poaching and illegal fishing.

Another new development at Kinloch Rannoch has been the establishment of a timeshare scheme, based upon the Kinloch Rannoch Hotel. A series of buildings have been erected, carefully landscaped amidst old pine trees, and they offer accommodation of a very high standard.

Accustomed as we are to the damp rigours of most Scottish self-catering properties, the Rannoch flats and apartments seem like paradise. After a hard day in the hills, walking and fishing, it is wonderful to return in the evening to a steaming sauna and a well-equipped, modern kitchen.

Our most disastrous Rannoch cottage was little better than a derelict shack, owned by an hotel in Aberfeldy. We had booked it for Easter in 1962, along with two friends from Glasgow. A plumber greeted us upon arrival with news that there was a problem with the water supply; but not to worry, he had arranged an alternative source — a pipe from the burn. Lighting was by pressure lamps and there was no cooker. For major culinary events, such as cooking the Easter turkey, one was expected to drive two miles along the road and use a cooker in a neighbour's outhouse.

The cottage was damp and cold and eventually, the ladies drove over to Aberfeldy to complain. They returned two hours later, laden with extra blankets, having been bustled rudely out the back door, out of sight of hotel guests. In spite of this welcome additional warmth, we slept fully dressed.

I am still puzzled, to this day, as to why we didn't simply demand a refund and leave; probably because we had all been looking forward to getting away so much that we were prepared to tolerate anything. And we did. In the evenings, after a dinner collected by the ladies from along the road, we huddled round the fire, playing bridge. The trick was to avoid being dummy. That poor unfortunate had to stoke the fire, pump the tilly lamps, dash upstream to unblock the water pipe, boil the kettle — on the open fire — and arrive back at the card table an exhausted, nervous wreck. Made for interested bidding.

Ann and I even managed to find a boat and ventured out fishing on Dunalister Reservoir, a shallow, flooded loch between Rannoch and Tummel, formed when the waters of Rannoch were impounded as part of the Pitlochry Hydro Electric Scheme. Which caused some difficulty. The loch is so new and shallow that underwater tree-stumps can still catch you unawares. I found myself aground in the middle of the loch, firmly wedged on one such stump, and the only way out of the problem was to leap overboard and shove. Both waders immediately filled and I caught my breath as freezing April waters began to stimulate sensitive nether regions. Gasping, chilled below and sweating above, I managed to wrestle the boat free. We decided to abandon fishing and head for home before I froze to death.

Our friends, who had gone to investigate the river, quickly decided that the call of the Kinloch Rannoch Hotel was far stronger than the call of April fishing. They were relaxing in front of a blazing fire when the door of the bar burst open and a local appeared: "Listen," he announced. "You will never guess what I have just seen." Everyone waited. "Two idiots, out on a boat on Dunalister in this blizzard. And do you know what, one of them is wading around in the middle of the loch, up to his waist in the water." Our friends laughed politely. "I wonder who on earth they are?" was their only contribution to the general merriment.

BRORA

OTHING is more predictable than the unpredictability of fishing. Each expedition is a new adventure, a new voyage of discovery. No matter how well you think that you know a river or loch, by the end of the day you will have acquired some piece of additional, vital information to add to your store of knowledge.

The tiny moorland lochan, where I cast once, whilst passing, and hooked and lost the biggest brown trout that I have ever seen. That fish is still there. The rowan tree, below which I know Grandad lies, a huge trout, at least 8lb in weight. The deep pot in Loch Croispol, Durness, where you will almost always catch a fish.

Over the years, this learning process helps anglers build up an encyclopaedic, mental reference book, full of important facts and figures: the best parts of the best pools; when certain lochs are most productive; what flies to use; underwater rocks, bogs to avoid. Small details, that make fishing a constant source of delight: a bank of yellow flag by a tiny burn; where mountain everlasting grow; secret otter greens; where we saw a wildcat; a peregrine's nest; rutting red deer; black-throated divers.

A lot of the places where Ann and I fish are in remote locations. Often at the end of a long, hard hike; and our greatest delight is finding new, unexplored waters to fish where, perhaps, the trout haven't seen an artificial fly for years.

We have tramped miles over mountain and moorland in search

of sport, and one of the joys of living and fishing in Scotland is that in spite of nearly forty years' trout fishing, we have at least another forty years to go before we can honestly say we know but a fraction of all the fishing available.

But not everyone likes their fishing rough, I am pleased to say, and the majority of anglers prefer more accessible locations, where, if nothing else, they can at least pronounce the name of the water or loch of their choice.

Loch Brora and the River Brora for instance, close to the most northerly coal-mining town on mainland Britain — although the mine, a private venture, closed a few years ago. The river rises close to the source of that other famous Sutherland salmon stream, the Naver, but Brora flows eastwards, collecting in the waters of its main tributary, the Black Water, at Balnacoil, then hurrying through Loch Brora, down to the cold, grey North Sea.

The upper river, above the loch, provides the best sport, and is rarely available to casual visitors. Fishing is let each year to the same people, many of whom have been coming to Brora for decades. Sutherland Estates, who own the salmon fishing rights, also rent out three superb shooting lodges along with the fishing; and these are the ideal location for a family party, or group of friends. Provided that they have at least £2,000 per week to spend on their pleasure.

Rods are sometimes available on the lower river, where Rockpool, half a mile from the sea, is open to the public for sea-trout in April, and from June onwards for salmon. In the right conditions, Rockpool can provide spectacular sport, particularly with sea-trout.

The town of Brora also boasts an excellent fishing hotel, The Royal Marine, close to Brora golf-course. Apart from good food and comfortable accommodation, The Royal Marine has a private swimming pool; the only hotel north of Inverness with such a facility. After a hard day tramping the hills in pursuit of brown trout, or fruitless hours on the banks of the river, trying to persuade salmon to rise, it is a great pleasure to plunge into the hotel pool and swim toils and tribulations away.

The most readily available game fishing for the visitor to this lovely area of Sutherland, is to be had on Loch Brora, but even there it is advisable to book well in advance to avoid disappointment. Brora is very popular.

There are really three lochs rather than one, almost separate, but joined by narrows, and after a wild winter, when the snows begin to melt, these narrows become rivers in their own right, with ice-cold waters pounding through on their three-and-a-half mile journey to the sea.

Loch Brora produces a good number of salmon each season, as well as Arctic char and some excellent brown trout; but the loch is most famous as a sea-trout fishery and from June until September, these wonderful, fighting fish provide outstanding sport.

Sea-trout are fidgety fish. Rarely staying in the same place long, as though never satisfied with their accommodation, forever charging about the loch, the problem for anglers is always the same: finding where they lie. And the best way to tackle that problem is not on the loch itself, but in the centre of town.

Rob Wilson's tackle shop in Brora has been welcoming anglers for more than fifty years. Although Rob, affectionately known as Mr Brora, has retired, you might still meet him in the shop that bears his name, now run by Colin Taylor, another well-respected and well-liked Brora angler. Both are always ready to give visitors the benefit of their experience and advice; and, at times, they may be able to arrange for newcomers to fish Loch Brora in company with a local angler. If given such an opportunity, agree quickly and say thank you. It could mean the difference between a red-letter day and an empty basket. Local knowledge is worth its weight in gold; or silver sea-trout.

Rob is full of stories and tales of fish landed and fish lost: a salmon of at least 30lb, lost in Madman Pool, the biggest fish Rob ever hooked; a fresh-run 12lb salmon, from Otter Pool, taken on a size 10 Peter Ross and a nine-foot Hardy Perfection rod: "Didn't do the rod much good."

My favourite tale, comes from Corner Pool, when Rob was fishing one cold March day: "I was about to start at the top of the pool when I happened to spot a flicker of movement close to the north bank. In the rush to get to the tail of the pool, I stumbled over a rock, and in putting out a hand to save a bad fall, dropped the rod and line into the water.

When I had recovered my equilibrium and picked the rod up, there was a fish on the end. Not only that, but he must have swallowed the large Garry Dog I had on the line, which must have floated down in an unrestricted way to him." The luck of salmon fishing.

Rob Wilson's reputation as a rod builder is unequalled in Scotland and perhaps the greatest test of his skill came in 1958. He had just completed work on a new two-and-three-quarter-ounce trout-rod, and had asked his brother, John, to try it out. Passing Bengie Pool, where Brora's largest salmon, a fish of 45lb, had been caught, John Wilson noticed a good fish rising and decided to have a throw at it. Mounting a size 8 Green Highlander, John cast out over the stream. At the eighth cast, the salmon grabbed.

One-and-a-half hours later, and after near disaster with the gaff, the head of which fell off, John Wilson managed to beach the great fish; a salmon of 40lb in weight, the second-heaviest fish ever taken from the river. Rob's trout rod had stood the sternest test.

Rob Wilson's courtesy and kindness is legendary and many years ago he indirectly helped my mother to hook her first salmon. It was a hot summer day, with the river showing its bones, and although fishing conditions were poor, Rob persuaded Mother to have a cast or two, rather than just sitting watching Father lashing away.

Mother was dressed more for sun-bathing than fishing, a home-made top being held in position whilst she tried to master the art of casting — much to the discomfort of an angler nearby; one of the old school: tie, sports jacket, plus fours, deer stalker and gillie. Because of inexperience and low-water conditions, she kept getting stuck on the bottom. Every time, Father never famous for his patience or length of temper, stamped down to free the fly; and he soon grew tired of this unrewarding activity and started to complain, bitterly.

When Mother got caught again, for the umpteenth time, rather than risk Father's mounting wrath, she gave the line a couple of vicious tugs, hoping he would not notice; and almost died of fright when an outraged salmon leapt from the water and made off upstream like a rocket.

Father rushed down and began yelling instructions; the gentleman and his gillie just stood, mouths open, hardly believing what they were seeing, as Mother struggled and splashed in the river, fighting the salmon with one hand whilst struggling to remain decent with the other. She eventually managed to get the salmon to the bank, and it turned on its side amongst the stones, gasping. For some reason, best known to himself, rather than quickly tailing the fish, Father chose that moment to give Mother a lecture

80

on the life-cycle of salmon, pointing out various aspects of salmon anatomy whilst doing so.

"Now dear, we don't have a gaff or net, so I will show you how to tail a salmon," he said, unctuously. The moment he touched the supposedly somnambulent salmon, the fish sprang to life, flapping wildly out of Father's grasp. Mother watched in horror as the fly fell from its mouth and it swam to freedom.

Mother always got annoyed when that story came up in conversation, and I made sure that it frequently did. And ever afterwards, when Father began to criticise my general angling inability, I could always stop him, instantly, by muttering under my breath the word "Brora".

Sutherland has a great sporting tradition. Not only because of its fine rivers, lochs and deer forests, but also as a centre of excellence for that other favourite Scottish pastime, golf. There are no less than eighteen golf-courses north of the Great Glen, the most famous of which is Royal Dornoch, half an hour's drive south from Brora.

There is almost a tradition of taking the family to the links, and introducing off-spring to the ancient game, as my own father did with me; very akin to the Scottish fishing tradition. Generation follows generation. Except, as far as fishing is concerned. With my father it was the other way round: I introduced him to angling.

One evening, when his golf match had been cancelled, he decided to drive down and collect me from the river. I was on Lyne Water at the time, a tributary of the River Tweed. I was fishing a lovely pool, at Flemington, and saw Father park the car. After a few minutes, he got out and wandered over: "Here, son, give me a shot at that," he said, and I passed him the rod.

That was it. I don't think Father played more than a couple of games of golf thereafter and he spent the next twenty years in pursuit of trout, salmon and sea-trout; never happier than when he was waist-deep, regardless of time of year or weather.

Golf and fishing are the national sports of Scotland, for both male and female, and I remember Mother, who was also a moderate golfer, fishing on a river adjacent to a golf-course, avoiding the balls flying past her head, many of which flew straight into the river.

She was watching a poor demented man, obviously having a bad day, hacking his way up the fairway towards her. His third shot was a wild slice, whistling just past Mother's left ear, splashing into the river. Eventually, he arrived at her side and, exasperated, flung his clubs down the bank and exclaimed crossly: "Here, lady, for God's sake, let's do a swap; you have these damned clubs and let me have your fishing rod. There must be a better way of spending life than what I'm doing."

Mother also had her bad days, fishing. When she was new to the gentle art she spent a lot of her time climbing trees, to retrieve misjudged casts, rather than bother Father. Often, in order to preserve peace, she would wander off in the opposite direction, to keep out of trouble. Which is how she came to find herself in such an embarrassing position. As I told her later, she only had herself to blame.

A particularly vicious back-cast entangled her cast, high in the branches of a nearby, unclimbable tree. Not having taken any spare flies, Mother determined that the only thing to be done, was to get the cast down, somehow. Pondering, she struck upon a brilliant idea. Reverse the rod, hook the reel over the branch, then pull it down. Two minutes later, Mother was holding half a trout rod. The butt section, having separated from the rest, complete with reel, was hanging above her head, next to the cast, out of reach.

In a final, ill-considered act of desperation, she tried to knock the butt section clear, using the remaining two sections as a spear. The middle section parted company next, landing neatly between two branches, and Mother was left staring at the tip section, contemplating disaster.

Fortunately, the head keeper arrived before Father, and he managed to sort out the mess. Mother stood on his shoulders and between the pair of them, amidst much shouting of directions and staggering about, the rod was brought down and reassembled.

When Father appeared, five minutes later, he was confronted by a scene of bucolic bliss: "Any luck, Mima?" he inquired. "No, Jack, absolutely nothing doing. Very quiet," she replied shamelessly.

I was never much good at golf, and lacked patience and co-ordination; but I once caught a pound trout on a Dunlop 65 golf-ball, and it happened like this. Near to where I live, in Caithness, there is a small loch, ideal for a quick cast if time is short. The loch is very weedy and fishing restricted to only a few clear patches; but there are some super trout to be had, deep bodied and golden in colour. I waded out, concentrating on casting towards the weeds, where I had seen a good fish rise, when a glint of white under the water caught my eye. Curious, I began scrabbling about with my foot, to see what it was. A golf-ball. Never one to look a gift horse in the mouth, I began kicking it ashore, at the same time trailing the flies in the water behind me.

Just as I was about ashore, I bent down to pick up the ball, getting a wet sleeve in the process. And at that precise moment, a fish grabbed.

I got such a shock that I toppled over sideways, ending up chest deep in freezing water. May in the Highlands is not warm. The fish was still on, and I had the golf-ball firmly clutched in my left hand, so I landed them both. Staggering to my feet, soaking but triumphant, I was greeted by loud clapping from the far bank. Three local anglers had been watching the pantomime with great enjoyment, and I have yet to live it down. When I tried to explain to them about the golf-ball it only made matters worse.

A few miles south from Brora, past the Duke of Sutherland's monstrous French-château fantasy castle at Dunrobin, is the town of Golspie, whose name derives from the old gaelic word meaning the "place of the strangers" and although evidence is sparse, it is thought that the strangers in question were Vikings.

During the eighth century the Vikings invaded and eventually controlled the area, which is the origin of its present name, Sutherland, the Viking "South Land". They integrated with the Picts, the "painted men", finally absorbing them and their culture completely, leaving behind only robbed brochs, broken hill-forts and a few stone carvings as evidence of the Picts' passing.

Integration was a Viking way of life; usually by force, rather than by persuasion. Fierce, ruthless men like Earl Seiguard of Orkney who died near Dornoch. He had just won a battle with one of the local earls to whom he wished to teach some manners, although the reason for the fight is unclear; but the Vikings never needed much of an excuse to fight.

One of the less endearing habits of the time, was to remove the head of the principal adversary, and carry it back to their castle, as a grisly trophy of war. Earl Seiguard, following tradition, severed the head, tied the bloody object to his saddle, and leapt aboard. In doing so, he grazed his leg on an exposed tooth of his victim, and such a trivial scratch was ignored. A few days later, Earl Seiguard died of blood poisoning. Heaven knows what his victim had been eating before the battle, but it ended Seiguard's reign of terror, permanently.

I can't leave this part of the world without relating a story about another, less grisly trophy, carried home from Sutherland; and the link it had with a polluted, southern stream, the White Cart, which empties into the Clyde estuary.

The Cart passes through the old mill town of Paisley, one of the principal reasons for its sorry state, and I was astonished one morning to open my *Scotsman* and read the headline: "Sea-trout return to the Cart".

A few days later, talking about this remarkable event to Tony Sykes, a friend from Bridge of Weir, I discovered the truth. Yes, sea-trout had indeed returned to the murky river Cart but not via the Clyde as everyone thought. They had travelled by car.

One of Tony's friends, Robin Whiteford, had been fishing in Sutherland and had caught some nice fish, including salmon and sea-trout. He also lived at Bridge of Weir, and on his way home through Paisley, late at night, he stopped on the old bridge. Taking two, freshly caught Highland sea-trout, he placed them on the mud flats below the bridge, where they were found the next morning. The papers were full of the story, sea-trout return to the River Cart. Learned letters, both for and against, bristled with information about how such an event could have occurred.

No one suspected the truth. The fish had never been anywhere near the Clyde. They were both North Sea silver, straight from Loch Brora.

UIST AND BENBECULA

T THE southern end of the Outer Hebrides lie three of the most lovely islands in the world: North Uist, Benbecula, and South Uist. The western edge of these Atlantic gems are fringed by wonderful, white, shell-sand beaches, backed by flower-bright, green machair plains; the east coast is rugged and inhospitable, bounding a trackless land, confronting mainland Scotland over the stormy Minch, beyond Cuillin on Skye.

But the most remarkable aspect of the Uists and Benbecula is the amazing number of freshwater lochs. North Uist is almost more water than land; Benbecula, a sparkling silver-blue maze; whilst the South Uist machair plains are adorned with some of Europe's finest sea-trout and brown trout lochs. But to believe it, you really must go there and see for yourself.

I did, for the first time in 1979, when we spent a family fishing holiday in the Hebrides; and we have been returning regularly ever since, constantly drawn back by the magic spell the Outer Hebrides cast over all who set foot upon her romantic shores.

All our family fish. The Chinese call it brainwashing. I call it common sense. From earliest years, each of our four children have been introduced to the gentle art and they are all still keen anglers. Consequently, when it came to deciding upon holiday locations, there were rarely arguments. The only problem was deciding where to go: Orkney, Caithness, Ross-shire, Sutherland or the Outer Isles?

Our first daughter, Lewis-Ann, sometimes complained: "Why can't we be like normal families and go to France or Greece?" she would moan. So one year, in deference to her wishes, we spent two, troutless weeks on the Loire coast. Lewis-Ann sat under a huge umbrella, fully clothed, complaining bitterly about being too hot. Teenage girls are like that.

Driving south from Lochmaddy in 1979 brought instant joy. Everywhere we looked, around every corner, over every rise, a seemingly endless array of lochs and lochans beckoned. Moorlands, mountains and hills crowded round on every side; seas shimmered azure, emerald, green and blue in August sunlight; the scent of peat smoke filled the air and we drove through a landscape that had remained almost unchanged for a thousand years. Tiny, patchwork, coastal fields were centred by small, four-square-to-the-wind crofts, some still turf-thatched; proprietorial, black-eyed sheepdogs snapped angrily at our car's wheels as we passed. Red-rust tractors parked, perched on downward-facing slopes, for easy starting. A woman cut a field of golden oats, the old way, using a hand sickle.

Our accommodation was in a caravan, close to the principal town of Benbecula, Balivanich. Of all the islands, Benbecula shows great evidence of change, because of the presence of a military base associated with the Royal Artillery rocket range on South Uist.

An airport was established at Balivanich during the Second World War, when, to improve inter-island communications, the South Ford, to South Uist, was bridged. After the end of the war Balivanich expanded as a "military zone", becoming the southern island's administrative centre; headquarters of Comhairle nan Eilean, the Outer Hebrides local government agency.

For two blissful weeks we explored the islands: fishing, swimming, wandering over moorlands to distant trout lochs and seaweed-fringed pools, alive with silver sea-trout. Buzzard, golden eagle and harrier shadowed our way; curlew piped from spagnum tussocks; soft, seemingly endless sunny summer days amidst a peaceful, glorious world.

North Uist is circled by a most convenient road which gives easy access to some marvellous beaches: the magnificent sweep of Valley Strand, guarded by deserted Valley Island; Traigh Leathann, by Claddach Kirkibost and Kirkibost Island; small, secret coves, at Scolpaig, Raikinish and Hougharry; near the Balranald Nature Reserve, home of rare red-necked phalarope and grating corncrake.

Within this encircling road, lie a series of superb brown trout and sea-trout lochs: Scadavay, with shores that meander round the moor for a distance of more than fifty miles; full of fishy points and promontories, reputed to contain 365 islands. One for every day of the year, with many of these islands hosting small lochs of their own.

The best salmon system on North Uist also lies here: Loch Skeltar, which exists under the road, past rocky Eilean Leiravay to the sea in Loch nam Madadh. Until recently, a salmon farm inhibited fishing in Skeltar, but this enterprise has since ended and salmon once more have freedom of access to their traditional spawning grounds.

A single track divides North Uist, from north to south, built in 1845 to provide employment during the terrible potato famine that ravaged Ireland and the Highlands of Scotland in the mid-nineteenth century. To the west of this road are the principal sea-trout waters: Struban, Dusary, Trosavat and Hosta. But the most exciting sea-trout fishing is to be found further afield, in distant sea-pools around the coastline; and one morning, leaving the ladies by a roadside lochan, Blair and I walked south from the A867 to Oban Sponish sea-pools, on the north shore of Loch Eport; a hard, circuitous hike, tramping for two hours over wet moorlands round Scadavay's ragged shores.

Oban Sponish is a long, narrow, tide-marked inlet, guarded from the sea by a rock bar. When the tide rises, cold waters flood in, bringing with them hard-fighting sea-trout which dash through the brackish, salt waters, sending waves swirling and anglers' hearts racing. Outstanding sport amid outstanding surroundings. Worth every soggy step of the way.

Men have been pursuing North Uist sea-trout for hundreds of years and the island is rich in sites of archaeological interest; brilliantly described by Dr Erskine Beveridge in his definitive book, *North Uist: its Archaeology and Topography*, published in 1911. The remains of duns, brochs, stone circles, burial chambers and standing stones lie scattered throughout the island. In Loch nan Geireann, between Beinn Dhubh Shollais and Crogary Hills, in the north is Eilean an Tighe, where archaeologists discovered the remains of what is probably the oldest pottery workshop in Western Europe.

Apart from historical interest, Geireann is also of great interest to the angler, offering the best of all worlds. The loch contains salmon, sea-trout and brown trout, with each species preferring certain areas: salmon in one place, other areas where you are more likely to catch sea-trout, and always, throughout the whole length, brightly marked, wild brown trout.

At Cleetraval, in the west of North Uist, there is a well-preserved Neolithic burial chamber, where quantities of pottery, probably made at Geireann, were found. A cairn, later surrounded by an Iron Age fort, marks the ancient grave; and at Carinish, before the causeway to Benbecula, are the ruins of one of the oldest churches in Scotland, Teampull na Trionaid, established in the early years of the thirteenth century.

My favourite Benbecula loch is Ba Alasdair, at the south end of the island; it lies to the north of a narrow, twisting track that leads north and then eastwards from the B891; about fifteen minutes' easy walk from the road. A brackish loch, into which sea-trout charge, when the tide is right.

Linked to Ba Alasdair by a feeder stream, just north over the hill at the head of the loch, there is an absolutely classic trout water, known locally as Bluebell Loch. In spring and early summer, some of the little islands here are a stunning mass of bluebells. A beautiful place. No people.

Blair and I also walked out to another, superb loch where we had splendid sport, Scarilode; about two hours' walk along a good track from Market Stance, past Rueval, where Charles Edward Stewart lay waiting for Flora Macdonald, prior to his flight from the Hebrides.

Benbecula and the Uists are famous for their association with Bonnie Prince Charlie, immortalised in "The Skye Boat Song". We visited many of the places associated with the fugitive, during his travels round the Outer Hebrides after the disaster at Culloden in 1746, including the South Uist birthplace of Scotland's most noted heroine, Flora Macdonald.

On the morning of 21 June 1746, Flora Macdonald left Prince Charles Edward Stewart's hiding place at Corrodale on South Uist; a cave, close to the cliffs, behind the mountain called Beinn Mhor. Her destination was Nunton, Benbecula, and her mission, to acquaint Lady Clanranald with details of a desperate scheme for the Prince's escape.

The fugitive and his boatmen had been washed ashore at Rossinish on Benbecula, in April, after a night of violent storms in the Minch:

"They came to an uninhabited hut where they made a fire to dry their clothes, for all of them were wet through to the skin, and an old sail was spread upon the bare ground, which served as a bed for the Prince, who was very well pleased with it and slept soundly."

News of the Prince's arrival was brought to Nunton on Sunday, 27 April; but one of Clanranald's dinner guests that night was the Rev John MacAulay, a presbyterian minister and loyal supporter of King George. MacAulay sent word to his father in Harris, and the hunt was up.

During the following weeks, the Prince travelled the Outer Hebrides in search of a means of escape; the Island of Scalpay, near East Loch Tarbert; Loch Seaforth and Stornoway; back to Loch Seaforth; Loch Uskevagh on Benbecula; landing at Corrodale on 14 May.

When Flora Macdonald presented herself at the south ford, before making the hazardous journey across the sands to Benbecula, the soldiers guarding the passage became suspicious and Flora was arrested and closely questioned. Eventually, and probably because the Commanding Officer was Flora's step-father, she was allowed to continue, and given papers authorising her journey, along with her servant, Neil MacEachan, and her maid, Betty Burke.

Whilst Flora and Lady Clanranald prepared the disguise Prince Charles was to adopt as Flora's maid, Betty Burke, the Prince was brought to Rossinish, and a boat organised with oarsmen, to carry the party "Over the sea to Skye".

Meanwhile, General George Campbell, with a force of some 1,500 men had crossed the north ford, from North Uist to Benbecula; two warships lay off the coast and the commander, Captain Scott, added a further 700 men to the hunting party.

On 27 June, Captain Ferguson of HMS *Furnace*, indefatigable pursuer of Prince Charles, slept at Nunton. Lady Clanranald, along with her daughter and Flora, were at Uskevagh, preparing for the Prince's departure. Lady Clanranald returned to Nunton, where she kept Captain Ferguson busy, adroitly evading all questions as to where she had been.

At about eight o'clock on the evening of 28 July, the Prince, disguised as Betty Burke and wearing a "flower'd linen apron gown", escaped from the Benbecula rowed by six strong men and accompanied by Flora Macdonald and faithful Neil MacEachan.

The party landed safely next day near Monkstadt on Skye. Allan Macdonald of Kingsburgh, Flora Macdonald's future husband, was a guest in the house at the time, and took food and drink to the Prince, still disguised as Betty Burke, and hiding on the hill. As he approached, the Prince prepared to defend himself, but calmed when Allan said: "I am Macdonald of Kingsburgh come to serve your Highness."

For her part in the daring escapade, Flora Macdonald was taken prisoner and, for a year, lay incarcerated on a troopship in Leith Roads in the Firth of Forth, before being taken to London, where she was sent to the Tower. Throughout her ordeal, Flora's spirit and character endeared her to everyone who met her until she was released under the Act of Indemnity in 1747.

She married Allan Macdonald in 1750 and now lies at rest in the churchyard at Kilmuir, near Duntulm Castle; beneath a white granite, Iona cross, and her winding sheet, the same sheet that softened Charles Edward Stewart's rest during his first night on Skye.

Neil MacEachan, a school teacher from the village of Howbeg on South Uist, remained with Prince Charles throughout all his subsequent adventures and wanderings in Scotland; and he accompanied Charles Edward on the final escape to France.

Shortly after his arrival in France, Neil married and the couple settled at Sedan, where their son, Jacques Etienne Joseph Macdonald was born in 1765. Like so many of his ancestors, Jacques "went for a soldier", and during the turbulent times of the French Revolution, quickly gained fame and fortune. In 1798 Jacques Etienne was appointed Governor of Rome and in 1809 Napoleon elevated his Celtic general to the status of Marshall of France.

However, Jacques Etienne never forgot his Hebridean origins and in 1826 set off on the long, difficult journey to his father's home at Howbeg. Before returning to France, he filled a box with earth and stones from his ancestral lands. When he died in 1840, the box joined him in his grave.

One of the principal problems facing anglers fishing on Benbecula and the Uists, is knowing where to begin; there are so many fine waters to choose from and never enough time to do proper justice to more than a handful.

Our first holiday to the islands helped solve that problem, and provided great help in future years. Blair, our oldest son, was entranced by the islands, and after university study and a BSc, he accepted employment with the Ministry of Defence, as a computer scientist at the RA South Uist rocket range.

Of even greater importance, he became Secretary of the South Uist Angling Club. Thus, in one, glorious fell swoop, we had not only first-hand, first-class information about island fishing locations, but also assured board and lodging when we arrived.

Blair worked on the islands for a number of years and I confess that I envied him. Shortly after his arrival, I telephoned to make sure he had settled in and all was well: "How are you, Blair?" was as far as I got. "Dad, it's wonderful. Every morning when I go to work, I see the mountains of Harris to the north, Cuillin and Skye eastwards, and the hills of Barra to the south. Caught a marvellous sea-trout last night . . ." Blair was fine.

That being the case, Ann and I quickly arranged to visit our son, to see his new home — and have a few casts; and Blair took me to where he had landed his sea-trout, in the sea-pool between Clett headland and Rubha Glas, over the golden sands at Geireann.

At low tide, sands are exposed and it is possible to walk out to the sea-pool. Best to travel with a local, because there are quicksands; and you should check tide times carefully before setting out. On our visit, Blair asked Graeme Longmuir to be our guide.

Graeme is chaplain at Strathalmond School in Perthshire, and he has a house on North Uist to which he escapes at every available opportunity. He knows every inch of the islands and, even better, is the proud owner of a huge Irish wolfhound. The dog bounded ahead across the shifting sands. Blair and I followed carefully in its footsteps, mightily encouraged.

When we arrived, Atlantic waves were breaking over a rock bar, surging with each swell through a narrow channel into the pool. The sea was emerald green, crested snow-white, and the water was myriad-coloured; reflecting golden sandy shallows, with shades from green hills and blue skies shimmering across the surface. The pool was packed with salmon and sea-trout, tearing round like mad things, splashing and leaping, throwing themselves out of the water in spectacular displays. In spite of all my best efforts, they remained in their domain, although Blair caught two; but just seeing them, and just being there, was reward enough.

The three islands have distinctive characteristics with the best of the game fishing being on South Uist. The word "best" is a relative term: all the islands offer wonderful sport. However, the machair lochs of South Uist are amongst the finest trout lochs in the world. They have a high pH level, rich in shell-sand lime, and are shallow, warming up quickly in the early months of the season. Because of the quality and quantity of available food, trout grow rapidly and fight hard.

Stilligarry is my favourite machair loch; a shallow straggle of bays and corners where good fish lurk. One Easter, whilst visiting Benbecula, my thoughtful daughter-in-law, Barbara, suggested a fishing picnic to Stilligarry. Early April in the Hebrides can be wild, but we always make it a rule that, if we have decided to go, then we go, regardless of weather conditions.

That Monday morning was particularly wet and windy, with a grey mantle of mist shrouding the slopes of Hecla and Beinn Mhor. The mist also shrouded the fish and we thrashed away mightily, to no avail. One by one, the member of Clan Sandison retired hurt. Left alone in solitary splendour, I could see them crouched behind the car, the flash of a hip-flask indicating that inner man and inner woman were being warmed.

I fished on, more as an act of defiance than in the hope of catching anything; and just as I was about to surrender a fish rose, as they always do in these circumstances, far beyond my reach. Not expecting much action, I hadn't bothered to put on boots, let alone waders. But I was determined to land a fly over that trout's nose, so I waded out, regardless of the freezing water, soaked to the knees.

The moment my fly touched the surface, the fish grabbed, greedily. I stumbled shorewards, praying the hook would hold, and after a considerable struggle, managed to beach a fine trout, just under 2lb in weight.

Triumphantly, I carried him to the car. "Fair weather anglers, the lot of you," I announced unctuously demanding immediate refreshment for my efforts.

Lochboisdale Hotel is the fishing centre of South Uist, famous for its public bar, which measures about forty feet in length; required to accommodate whaling crews, returning thirsting from the South Atlantic. Even today, I have never seen the bar empty. Busy places, bars, in the Hebrides.

A well-loved picture dominates the bar, held in almost religious awe: a photograph of the SS *Politician*, the vessel which ran aground off Eriskay during the Second World War, cargoed with 20,000 cases of whisky; not all of which went to the bottom when the boat eventually sank.

Compton Mackenzie used the incident as the theme for his superb book, *Whisky Galore*, and in 1989 a company was formed to salvage anything remaining intact in no. 5 hold. It is hoped, by all concerned, that the hold contains, unbroken, 2,000 cases of the historic "water of life".

Salvage work is expected to start in earnest in spring 1990, when, by lucky chance, I shall be spending the whole of June on South Uist. Should the weather be unkind, or fish reluctant to rise, then I am sure that I will be able to find plenty of other sea-borne activities to keep me fully occupied; and, hopefully, merrily amused.

ASSYNT

INDY Loch Assynt lies a few miles from the coast, near the picturesque fishing village of Lochinver; surrounded by a ridge of mountains eleven miles in length, none of which drop below 2,000 feet, crowned by Sutherland's highest peak, mighty Ben More Assynt.

The best way to fully appreciate this magnificent landscape is to climb the long grey shoulder of Canisp (2,700 feet), south of Loch Assynt, an easy three-and-a-half hour walk to the summit and back. Ann and I last made the journey on a cold April day in 1987, leaving the car by the shores of little Loch Awe, our two dogs bounding excitedly ahead.

On reaching the snowline, the weather deteriorated and after crunching knee-deep through frozen drifts for half an hour, we decided discretion was more sensible than ill-considered valour and made our way back down. By the time we reached the car, Canisp had disappeared amidst the storm.

However, from the summit of Canisp, on a clear day, you will be rewarded by one of the most stunning views in Scotland. To the south, Inverpolly National Nature Reserve, crowded with dramatic mountains: Suilven, Stac Polly, Cul Mor and Cul Beag; and in the distance, beyond the crags of Coigach, the peaks and pinnacles of Fisherfield in Wester Ross. Northwards across Loch Assynt, the hills of North-West Sutherland line the horizon: Quinaig, Arkle, Foinaven and Ben Stac. Westwards, glimmering on the green Atlantic lies misty Skye, and in the distance, Lewis, the "heather isle" of the Outer Hebrides.

Norman MacCaig, one of Scotland's finest modern poets, knows this area well; and as a keen trout fisherman has explored Assynt more thoroughly than most. MacCaig dramatically captures the spirit of this wonderful land in his poem, "Musical Moment in Assynt".

He sings the praises of Cul Mor, saying: "And God was Mozart when he wrote Cul Mor." Suilven, that finest of all Sutherland mountains, is described as: "One sandstone chord that holds up time in space."

The name Suilven is Norse in origin. As the Vikings rowed their warships round the north of Scotland, past Cape Wrath, their "turning point", down the ragged west coast of their "South Land", they saw Suilven as a single, dramatic pillar; and they named it Sul Val, the pillar mountain.

This pillar is Caisteal Liath, the grey castle, highest point on Suilven; and although Suilven is only a modest 2,399 feet in height, its isolation and stark setting makes it appear much higher, rearing majestically from the surrounding moorlands in solitary splendour.

Anglers sing the praises of Loch Assynt with similar fervour to that expressed by Norman MacCaig. The loch is full of wild brown trout; where a basket of thirty trout is the rule, rather than the exception. Assynt is so heavily populated with small fish, it is considered good policy to reduce their numbers; fewer mouths mean more food all round, and larger trout.

But Assynt also holds ferox of great size in its dark depths. Fish of more than 10lb in weight have been caught, generally by autumn anglers, trolling for salmon. Recently, three ferox weighing over 20lb were taken in a single day. The first, a fish of 5lb, was displayed in the hotel by its proud captor, being much admired by guests. Ten minutes later another angler arrived with a fish of 5lb 8oz. Shortly afterwards, Mr Smith from Edinburgh came in with a ferox weighing 8lb 8oz.

Assynt is a good salmon loch with upwards of sixty fish being caught most seasons. Salmon travel from the sea at Lochinver, up the River Inver, into the six-mile-long loch. Sometimes, even further, fighting their way through tiny Lonnan Burn to island-clad Loch Awe.

Many a trout angler has had a red-letter day on Loch Awe, suddenly encountering a sea-liced silver salmon whilst trout fishing; then having the thrill and excitement of playing the fish on light tackle.

Anglers who like exercise with their fishing are well provided for at Assynt. The surrounding hills, compass and map country, have dozens of marvellous trout lochs, most of which are full of sparkling little fish; and a few which hold much heavier specimens.

Discovering where the big fish lie is part of the pleasure of fishing in this area. Tiny waters, 2,000 feet up, can produce trout of 3lb. Drag on the climbing boots, stride off into the hills, and find out for yourself. On the way, you should also discover one of Scotland's most spectacular waterfalls, Eas Coul, "the maiden's tresses", four times higher than Niagara Falls.

The centre of angling activity in Assynt is Inchnadamph Hotel, owned and run by one of the north's most colourful characters, Willie Morrison: expert fisherman and raconteur, always ready to help, advise, and, when necessary, commiserate with his angling guests. And should you happen to be archaeologist, geologist, botanist, ornithologist, indeed any other sort of -ologist, then Inchnadamph National Nature Reserve will please and delight.

A limestone outcrop, extending from Durness at Cape Wrath to Broadford on the Island of Skye, surfaces behind the hotel and hosts an astonishing array of rare plants: Don's twitch grass, named after George Don, Forfar botanist; hakweed, stone crop, whortle-leaved willow, purple and mountain saxifrage, Norwegian sandwort, alpine saw-wort and frog orchid.

Deep caves and passages have been cut into the limestone by streams flowing from Ben More Assynt: by the glen of Traligill Burn, the Vikings' "Trolls' Gill" or giants' ravine; Noc nan Uamh, the "hill of the caves", Allt nan Uamh, the "burn of the caves". Some of these caves produced animal remains reputed to be 10,000 years old.

After Ann and I abandoned our assault on Canisp, we visited Traligill, and when another snowstorm swept down the mountain, we scuttled to safety in a convenient cave. Very comfortable we were too, as no doubt were the first occupants, Neolithic men and their families.

One of our favourite Assynt lochs lies a mile or so beyond the caves, and is known as the Gillaroo Loch, the name being derived from a species of Irish trout which inhabit limestone loughs such as Neigh and Mask. These fish have developed remarkably tough gullets due to the high proportion of fresh water crustacean in their diet. A similar species used to inhabit Loch na Moal Choire, long since fished out, but the loch still provides sport with native wild brown trout.

A more notable captive was taken at Assynt in 1650: James Graham, Marquis of Montrose. Montrose was a staunch loyalist and one year after Cromwell and his gang removed King Charles I's head from his shoulders, Montrose landed in Orkney, intent upon restoring the murdered king's son to the throne.

Montrose was defeated at the Battle of Carbisdale, on the Kyle of Sutherland, and fled westwards to Assynt. Neil Macleod, eleventh chief of the Assynt Macleod's, offered the fugitive refuge at Ardvreck, his castle in the loch; but once he had Montrose safely under his roof, Macleod imprisoned him in the castle dungeon. The government had offered £20,000 for Montrose and Macleod claimed that reward; but his perfidious abuse of the age-old tradition of Highland hospitality brought him only 400 bolls of oatmeal, and the eventual ruin of his clan.

Montrose's reward for his loyalist sympathies was more immediate. He was tied to the back of a horse and taken to Edinburgh, where he was tried, convicted and hanged. Various parts of his body were sent round Scotland, to remind his countrymen of the consequence of rebellion.

In 1660, Charles II was restored and Macleod found himself in prison, where he lay, without trial, for three years; whilst his neighbour, Mackenzie of Seaforth, dismembered his estates. Dismembered bits of poor Montrose were collected and then buried with honour in St Giles, the High Kirk of Edinburgh.

When Ann and I first visited this area, we followed the same route as luckless Montrose, travelling south from Caithness, over the Ord to the Kyle of Sutherland, past Lairg, then up Strath Oykle. At the watershed, by the track that leads northwards to Ben More Lodge and Loch Ailsh, we had our first, unforgettable glimpse of Assynt and Inverpolly.

Instantly we fell in love with the area and have been returning regularly ever since. When the slings and arrows of outrageous everyday life buffet our heads, we escape to Assynt, even if only for a long weekend, and always return refreshed, perspective regained.

However, that day, we were also on our way to battle, although of a less deadly kind and with less deadly consequences. The scene of our fight was the old school house at Elphin, converted and refurbished by Highland Regional Council into a school holiday centre. A party from Wick High School were booked in for the weekend.

There were a number of girls in the party and at the last minute the female teacher who was to chaperone them dropped out. Which, in retrospect, said a lot for her common sense; but a lady was still required and because our daughter was there, my wife Ann was dragooned into duty. Unsuspecting, and being a decent, trusting sort of man, I foolishly agreed to tag along and help.

The noise fifteen excited youngsters make has to be heard to be believed. Long after lights out, screams of feigned terror rang round the building as boys and girls fought the age-old battle of the sexes; until the senior master present, Bill Oliver, "the gonk", roared at them to keep quiet. His command brought instant silence. I was not surprised. The gonk scared the hell out of me, so his effect on the children must have been even greater; but it was a super weekend, in spite of everything; hill-walking, climbing, canoeing, and I even managed to drag some of the boys and girls off on a fishing expedition.

Ann did most of the cooking, assisted occasionally, by the young ladies and teachers. I washed-up a lot. Apart from the stunning beauty of the surrounding countryside, one of my most enduring memories of that weekend was always being last down for breakfast. I began to worry. Why did I take so long each morning? Was I really so slow and so old? Eventually, light dawned. I was the only member of the group who shaved. Everyone else was either too young or female, and all the teachers had beards.

Elphin lies close to the boundary between Sutherland and Ross-shire, and in days past there were frequent disputes between the two counties as to the exact position of the boundary line.

A famous attempt to resolve the matter is commemorated at Altnacealgach, "the burn of the cheat", a few miles north from Elphin. Two senior Ross-shire men were ordered to walk the boundary, as they knew it, being sternly warned before they set off: "Mind, your feet are on oath." When they returned, having taken in a fair part of Sutherland, they swore that their feet had never once left Ross-shire soil. Nor had they, because the old devils had filled their shoes with earth from Balnagowan in Easter Ross. They could claim, with a clear conscience, that their feet had never left Ross-shire soil.

This part of the world is never short of tales and stories, and the Altnacealgach Hotel, by the shores of Loch Borralan, was a good place to hear them. Was, because a few years ago the hotel burned down and has gone forever.

Happily, the stories live on, such as the visiting sportsman who, when boasting about his prowess with the gun, was easily put down by a local crofter: "Man, that is nothing. The other day I was out on the hill when I came upon a herd of four stags, and I shot five of them, just as easy as that."

I remember one evening in the bar, hearing a group of English anglers complaining bitterly. They had been lured miles into the hills by reports of a distant loch, full of superb fish that hadn't seen artificial fly or an angler for years. Not surprisingly, they returned fishless, exhausted and furious at having wasted the day and so much of their breath. After dinner, they lined the bar, talking loudly about the perfidy of Highlanders and bemoaning their ten-mile, fishless walk. A local, standing nearby, eventually intervened, saying: "Now gentlemen, if only you had the good sense to ask me first. I could have directed you to a loch that is right by the side of the road where you would have caught nothing all day."

South from Elphin, along the road to Ullapool, are the Knocknan cliffs, another famous Assynt limestone outcrop, and where the Moine Thrust, a geological feature, can be clearly seen. Before the Atlantic Ocean existed, 900 million years ago, Scotland was joined to America, and it was then that Torridon sandstone was formed.

These sandstones form the bulk of the stark Assynt peaks: Quinag, Canisp, Suilven and Ben More Assynt; and they are topped with sparkling quartz of the Moine Series, thrust to the surface by the tremendous geological forces which shook planet earth some 430 million years ago.

Close to the Inchnadamph Hotel, a monument commemorates the work of the two geologists who did most to unravel the secrets of these rock movements: Ben Peach and John Horne, colleagues of Archibald Geikie of the Geological Survey in Scotland in 1907.

Another Assynt man who knows these wild places, at all levels and in all weathers, is Tom Strang, mountaineer, author, angler, naturalist, ornithologist and quite a lot else besides; a man of boundless energy with great enthusiasm for Assynt and the outdoor life. Indoors as well, because Tom and his wife Ray run one of the most comfortable and welcoming holiday centres in the north, the Birchbank Activity Holiday Lodge at Elphin.

Birchbank caters for a maximum of ten guests at any one time, so individual attention is assured and just about every outdoor activity is provided, including cross-country skiing. Tom even has a photographic dark-room for guests' use; and for me, the greatest plus, a splendid sauna suite, complete with adjacent shower and rest area. Marvellous for relaxing aching muscles after a hard day in the hills.

Where to acquire the ache is never hard to find in Assynt. Stac Polly will always oblige. This perfect little mountain may only be just over 2,000 feet in height, but going up the south face, in my state of physical unfitness, you really know that you have had a climb, and regret all the long, glass-happy evenings of days past.

Stac Polly was the first real climb either of our dogs enjoyed. Or, at least, I think they enjoyed. Ann's animal is not really a dog, it is a Yorkshire terrier, something quite different. My golden retriever, Breac, is a proper dog. They both went galloping about the pinnacles like mad things. I envisaged myself staggering down, a dog under each arm, and roared them to heel.

Another climb guaranteed to set the pulse racing, is to the top of Suilven, and the walk out passes one of our favourite fishing locations, Fionn Loch, which lies below Suilven's towering heights. The path from Inverkirkaig is a delight, following the course of Kirkaig River, past deep, silent pools where silver salmon lie; by the roaring splendour of sixty-foot high Kirkaig Falls.

Fionn Loch, the "white loch" holds some fantastic wild brown trout, fish of up to 4lb and more in weight; and deeper down, ferox, caught by the old Scottish fishing method, trolling. Apart from the chance of filling the glass case, Fionn also has large stocks of more traditionally sized Highland trout, averaging 8-12oz, and as on Loch Assynt, large baskets are the rule rather than the exception.

The Sutherland and Ross-shire county boundary runs down the middle of the loch, touching the coast at the outlet of Kirkaig River, and Fionn collects in waters from hundreds of square miles, gathering them from as far away as Loch Borralan, at Atnacealgach, Urigill, Cama, the "crooked loch", and long, wind-swept Veyatie, below Cul Mor. Fionn receives them all, hurrying them seawards, over Kirkaig Falls to Inver Bay.

The principal town in this area is Ullapool, founded by the British Fisheries Society towards the end of the eighteenth century to exploit the shoals of herring that used to arrive each July. Sadly, these days are gone, and, it seems, Man's rapacious rape of the sea is now performing the same disservice to other species of white fish.

One of the main streets is Pultney Street, in honour of the Chairman of the British Fishery Society, also remembered on the other side of the country, in Caithness, where the society built the new fishing community of Pultneytown, on the south shore of Wick Bay.

Ullapool still flourishes as a fishing port, crowded with foreign vessels, known as Klondikers, using the port as a staging place for factory ships working the fisheries in and beyond the Minch. The number of different accents heard along the sea front would rival Oxford Street on a Saturday afternoon: Russian, Polish, French, German, Spanish, English and, of course, the native tongue of the Highlands, Gaelic.

Ullapool is guarded to the north by the mountains of Coigach, the "fifth part" of Ross-shire; and the busy town figures highly in the "escape from the rat-race stakes", being popular with our English cousins. The population is very cosmopolitan, most un-Highland, and there is plenty to keep everyone amused, even if you are not a game fisherman. If you are, then it is even nicer. There are some really splendid waters waiting for your first, well considered cast. A series of three fine lochs border the twisting little road that leads from Drumrunie out to the Summer Isles: Lurgainn, Bad a'Gahil and Oscaig.

The first two are good brown trout waters. Oscaig, owned by the Marquess of Linlithgow, is a splendid sea-trout loch. Of course, sea-trout never give themselves up easily; you have to know your loch and be prepared to hunt for where the fish lie; so be prepared for a lot of rowing, and a lot of finger-crossing on Oscaig. But if sea-trout refuse to co-operate, follow the outlet burn from Loch Oscaig, the river Garvie, and you will arrive at one of Scotland's most secluded and attractive beaches, the perfect place for a family picnic; and in the unlikely event of there being someone else there, fear not; walk over the headland to the east and you will find another, equally attractive, secret bay. Laze away a long summer day, lulled by the sound of green, white-fringed Atlantic waves, hundreds of miles old, endlessly washing golden sands. The fish will still be waiting in the lochs whilst you do; and tomorrow is another day.

GLADHOUSE

WAS a child in Edinburgh during the Second World War. On Guy Fawkes nights we burned an effigy of Mr Hitler and sang ribald songs about Gobbels, Goering and Himmler. Each year, as 5 November approached, my brother Ian and I scoured the streets, hunting for anything that would burn, begging at every door. Then a great fire was built in the middle of our wide, stone-cobbled street, and adults and children would gather round, cheering as hated Hitler burned. I didn't really understand what Guy Fawkes had to do with all this and was too embarrassed to ask. But if Guy Fawkes had almost succeeded in blowing up the Houses of Parliament, I concluded that he must have been a German spy. It seemed a reasonable explanation at the time and I continued to believe this until long after war ended and truth dawned.

We lived at No. 26 Wellington Street, close to London Road Gardens. Across the road, on waste ground, water storage tanks had been constructed, and at the end of hostilities they were drained. Boys crowded round to scoop out stickle-backs that floundered in the muddy shallows as the tanks emptied.

I imagine this is when I first became interested in fish, like so many other small boys; armed with a jamjar, clutching a net, insecurely tied to the end of a garden cane, carrying their unwelcome catch back to mother, wet to the knees and bursting with pride.

Edinburgh offered great fishing opportunities for wandering spirits. My brother and I haunted the lochs in King's Park, intent upon ever-larger prey: St Margaret's, weed-covered Dunsapie and delightful Duddingston were all within easy striking distance of home.

Duddingston was best. I rarely returned dry-shod from Duddingston, being certain that just one step further would put me amongst the fish. Never did. All I ever caught were wet feet and a thick ear from Father for returning home sodden, yet again.

Every time I look at Henry Raeburn's marvellous painting of "The Rev Robert Walker Skating on Duddingston Loch" I smile inwardly. He must have taken the odd tumble, for all his elegant, self-confident style. I wonder if his father ever greeted him quite so hotly when he arrived home, damp from Duddingston?

Another favourite venue was the pond in Inverleith Park, where we used to sail crudely constructed boats. We spent most of our time wandering round the banks whilst these ill-shaped craft drifted, keel up, from one side of the pond to the other.

Our finest moment came when Ian was given a "proper" yacht. It had a green and white painted hull, real sails, rudder and miniature block and tackle to set the rigging. However, we soon discovered why it had been abandoned; the keel was not large enough and in the slightest breeze the boat capsized. We tried various methods of increasing the yacht's stability, adding tons of lead weights to the base of the keel; until one day, in a strong wind, the unhappy vessel simply flopped over and sank out of sight forever.

The yacht was not the only thing I helped to sink in the pond. One Saturday morning, whilst fishing for anything daft enough to come my way, I saw three girls I vaguely knew — the way small boys know older girls — fishing from the stone jetty at the south end of the pond.

They were pupils at James Gillespie's High School for Girls and they were dressed in their school uniforms, as was the custom then: navy skirt, red blazer, topped by pill-box red hat. Older brother Ian, by that time beginning to take a more active interest in members of the opposite sex, was on speaking terms with the young ladies.

They were all chattering happily, splashing their nets in the water, and I felt excluded from the general mirth and hilarity. So, to reassert my presence, I crept up behind them and gave a sudden, ear-piercing screech.

Two of the girls fell sideways. The third, Ian's love, whose name was Helen, to my complete astonishment, jumped straight into the pond. The water was not deep, but Helen went right under. She struggled to her feet, bemused and frightened, and her friends hauled her out. I remember the skirt, clinging damply round her legs.

And that is about all I remember; for Ian and the girls, with single accord, rushed at me with such fury that I barely escaped with my life. No sense of humour, girls; but I gave Inverleith pond and Gillespie girls a wide berth for several weeks to come.

My route to Inverleith took me along the banks of the Water of Leith, via Canonmills. One bank of the river was lined with houses, known in Edinburgh as the Colonies, and the other had an earth path, bounded on either side by bushes and trees.

It was whilst walking along this path that I became aware of birds, flitting amongst the sparse branches; noticed how the robin's breast changed colour with changing seasons; learned the difference between male and female blackbirds.

I also became aware of brown trout. I used to walk down Rodney Street, past our local cinema, the Ritz, to Canonmills, where there was a grand clock mounted on a tower in the middle of the road; long since removed as a sop to the infernal, internal combustion engine. By the side of the bridge at Canonmills, steps lead down to a small, gravel-covered park, overlooking the river. My secret place. I would sit there for hours watching these little fish, turning and twisting in the current, occasionally rising to take a fly. Until my clock told me it was time to head for home.

Thus fly-fishermen are born, even in the middle of a great city, and that love of fishing has stayed with me throughout my life; a continual source of pleasure and enjoyment. Far better than money in the bank. Money comes and goes, but a love of fishing brings joy forever.

I discovered a lot of things at Canonmills that became important as I grew older: Robert Louis Stevenson's home at No. 1 Inverleith Terrace, close to the Royal Botanical Gardens, where the family lived in 1853. They didn't stay long because the house was cold and damp.

Stevenson was never very strong, physically, even as a child, and they quit Inverleith to move to more amenable, healthy surroundings at No. 17 Heriot Row, where Stevenson stayed for the next thirty years. It was at Heriot Row, cared for by his much-loved nurse, Crummy, that Stevenson discovered Leerie, the Lamplighter:

Now Tom would be a driver and Maria go to sea,
And my papa's a banker and as rich as he can be;
But I, when I am stronger and can choose what I'm to do,
O Leerie, I'll go round at night and light the lamps with you.

As my interest in birds grew, I began visiting the Royal Botanical Gardens regularly, passing Stevenson's house along the way. I would stand beneath trees for ages during cold, winter days, hand outstretched, waiting for robins and blue tits to alight and peck at proffered crumbs. I still feel their tiny claws on the edge of my palm.

Edinburgh is a remarkable city. Almost every house in both the Old and New Town, has some story to tell, and as a boy, wandering the sombre, grey streets, I would stop and peer at plaques, puzzling over the dark, stone-carved lettering. Who was he? What did he do?

I found the house where Chopin lodged, close to Canonmills, when he charmed Edinburgh society with his delicate playing and mystical melodies; Raeburn's studio, at 32 York Place, where he moved in 1795, the same year that young Robert Burns hit town; Walter Scott's home at 39 Castle Street, where most of the *Waverley* novels were written.

No. 45 George Street was special to me, because it was there that William Blackwood published his famous journal, *Blackwood's Edinburgh Magazine*; supported by John Wilson, using the pseudonym "Christopher North". Wilson, who was an unlikely Professor of Moral Philosophy at Edinburgh University, adopted the titles MA and FRS: Master of Angling, and Fisherman Royal of Scotland.

No doubt, in his quieter moments, Wilson cast a fly in Edinburgh's stream, the Water of Leith; and in what other European capital can you find such excellent fly fishing within a stone's throw of the city centre?

In recent years, fishing on the Water of Leith has been greatly improved by Lothian Regional Council's Department of Leisure

Services, and trout of up to 2lb 5oz have been caught. Even in my young days, trout of considerable size could be taken.

Near to Stockbridge, a laundry overhangs the Water of Leith, and I remember a relative of the owner telling me that from the managing director's window, one could look down and see a fish of at least 2lb, guarding its territory. Every time he called, he made straight for the window. To ensure his protégé was safe and well.

It is estimated that as many as 5,000 trout are taken each season from the Water of Leith, and from time to time, salmon attempt to run the stream: two fish reached the weir below Dean Bridge in 1977, although most are denied access by the lock gates at Leith Docks.

In the late 1940s and early 1950s I used to fish the Water of Leith above Balerno, with my father, and we always managed to return home with trout for supper. Fine eating they made. The smallest of flies, size 16 and 18, both dry and wet, mounted on the lightest of tackle, produced results. Crossing the fingers helped too.

In the days before I owned a trout-rod, as a special treat, our parents used to take us to Flotterstone and Glencorse Reservoir, in the Pentland Hills to the north of the Edinburgh/Biggar road. And if we were very good, behaved and did what we were told, we were treated to lemonade and cakes in Flotterstone Tea Rooms.

Glencorse fascinated me. When the valley was flooded, the chapel of St Catherine-in-the-Hopes was submerged; and it was said that the chapel bell could still sometimes be heard, sounding sullenly below the waves. Hearing the bell was reputed to be a warning of approaching doom and disaster. Ian and I used to hang over the reservoir wall, straining our ears, terrified that we might hear the bell toll, and yet willing it to ring. We needn't have worried. Before the chapel drowned, the bell was removed.

Glencorse is an L-shaped loch with an attractive, wooded island. The water is regularly stocked by Lothian Regional Council, with both brown and rainbow trout, and although the fish are not large, it is the ideal venue for an hour's sport. Only minutes from town.

There are a number of excellent trout lochs, all within easy reach of Edinburgh, where anglers will find good sport: Clubbiedean, Crosswood and Harperrig, Rosebery, Donolly and little Hopes Reservoir near Gifford, all administered by the council.

Other waters are privately owned: Bowden Springs, near Linlithgow, superb Linlithgow Loch, dominated by one of Scotland's most beautiful royal palace's; Loch Coulter, by Bonnybridge; the Maltings Fishery at Dunbar; Markle, on the outskirts of East Linton, where fish of up to 8lb have been caught.

All these lochs are easily accessible, both by public transport and by car, but when I was young in Edinburgh, owning a car was the exception rather than the rule. Few of my friends' fathers had cars. Our principal means of transport was either by foot — and we used to walk distances that would draw screams of horror from youngsters today — or bucketing along in style, aboard a tramcar.

During school holidays, my brother and I found a more leisurely means of getting round town: by horse and cart. We moved from Wellington Street to Claremont Crescent, shortly before Father returned from the War, and Ian and I quickly made friends with the person we deemed to be most important in our lives. The milkman.

Most days, after he had delivered our milk, we would join him on the rest of his round, helping to deliver cold bottles; frequently warmed by hot, sweet tea, splashed into half-pint bottles by friendly customers; luxuriating in pride of place, up front on the bench, urging the horse to greater speed.

However, one of my friends' fathers, Mr Hunter, did have a car, a large Humber Super Snipe, and I was frequently invited to join their party on weekend picnics in the surrounding countryside. Which is where I guddled my first brown trout.

A favourite picnic location was fifteen miles south from Edinburgh, near the little village of Eddlestone, on the road to Peebles. A minor road climbs from Eddlestone into the Meldon Hills, Black Meldon and White Meldon, and this track is bordered by a tiny, crystal-clear stream.

On hot summer Sundays we would splash in deep, cool pools; and then get down to the task of catching the small, brightly marked, red-spotted trout that dashed between our feet. I heard my first curlew at Meldon, calling hauntingly across the moor; saw my first owl, floating ghostlike through the car headlights one night as we returned home.

Mr Hunter sometimes produced a small trout-rod and tried for the larger fish that lived in a sizeable pond, formed by damming the burn; and it was there that I first attempted to master the intricacies of casting; and first heard that magical sound: the rackety clack of an earnest trout-reel in action. Thirty years later I returned to the Meldon Hills. They were just as charming. Full of happy memories.

You are never very far from good fishing in Edinburgh. Two of the most famous game fishing venues in the world lie only half an hour's drive away: glorious Loch Leven, in Kinross; and Tweed, Queen of Scottish rivers, flowing through magnificent Border lands, offering spectacular sport with salmon, sea-trout and brown trout.

But I must admit that my favourite lowland water is Gladhouse Reservoir. I never think of Gladhouse as man-made, because it looks so natural, and it is really a hill loch, although you may not realise it. It lies in the Moorfoot Hills at an altitude of 900 feet.

Gladhouse is also a nature reserve of considerable importance, and a marvellous place for seeing a great variety of birds, both resident and migrant; greylag and pink-footed geese arrive in vast flocks to spend their winter at Gladhouse. A super place.

I first visited Gladhouse in 1952, as a Boy Scout. When I shouldn't have. But it was late at night, about 2 a.m., raining, and we had to camp somewhere. We were on an adventure hike, from Edinburgh, and had been taken in an enclosed lorry, somewhere, and left to find our way home.

We found our bearings at Temple, by the light from the window of a cottage by the road. Inside, the lady of the house was ironing. At midnight. I still wonder why. We tramped on and eventually found ourselves at Gladhouse, where we decided to camp in a clump of wind-swept trees at the south end of the loch.

In the morning, before beginning the long hike back to Edinburgh, I marked the tell-tale rings of rising trout and made a mental note to return and investigate more thoroughly.

It was ten years, a wife and two children later before I did; and getting permission to fish Gladhouse was far more difficult than actually catching the blighters.

In those days, the good old 1960s, when Edinburgh City Council reigned supreme, there was a ballot system. If you wanted to fish Gladhouse, you applied, in writing, to the Water Department, giving the date you wished to launch your attack. All the names wishing to fish on the same day were put into a hat and, if you were lucky, your name might be pulled out. Democratic.

But Ann and I must have been very unlucky, because no matter how often we applied, our names were never drawn from the depths of the democratic civic hat. Being a trusting sort of person, it took me some time to realise what was happening; and what tactics I would have to adopt in order to be democratically selected.

I had a friend who worked with the Water Department, so I had a quiet word with him, explaining the problem, telling him the date we had requested in our most recent application. Surprise, surprise. At last, our name came out of the hat.

So we had our day on Gladhouse, a day in the best Sandison tradition. Ann was six months pregnant, the wind was blowing force eight, it was freezing cold and pouring. Eventually, we decided, against my better judgment, to get afloat. Within five minutes, we found ourselves fighting for our lives in the midst of the storm. All I could achieve on the oars was to keep the waves behind us as the boat whistled down the loch, hoping we would reach the shore before we were swamped. We ended up in an unmanageable heap of rods, lines, wet legs, wet bums, gasping on the shore, wondering what had hit us. And why we had been so stupid as to set out in the first place.

I dragged the boat clear, up the shingle bank, and we staggered to the shelter of a very high, immaculately groomed, privet hedge, to continue our argument about who had been to blame for the near-disaster.

Whilst sitting there, still arguing, I became aware of a noise: clip, clip, clip. I looked up. Above me, one of the estate workers was busy clipping the high hedge. He looked down and inquired politely: "Can I help you?"

I thought he would come down from the ladders he was obviously standing on, to talk to us. Instead, the head simply moved along the hedge-line and I was confronted by the largest man that I have ever seen — and I am no midget at six-foot four; but he towered above me.

He asked what the trouble was and I explained that we couldn't fish because of the strength of the gale; and I very much doubted whether or not I would be able to return the boat to its mooring place.

He suggested that we use a sea-anchor, and pointed to a huge concrete block on the shore, with a ring in the top. "What about

110

that?" he said, lifting it up with his fingers. I thanked him and tried to lift the block. I couldn't raise it from the ground, using both hands and all my strength.

The giant eventually offered to help me row the boat back to the mooring bay and I accepted his offer with alacrity. Failure to return the boat to its proper place would probably have meant beheading outside the City Chambers. At least.

It was a trip that I will never forget. We started with one oar each, and spent the first ten minutes going round in circles. I couldn't match his strength. Eventually, my companion took both oars and rowed us back as easily as though we were afloat on Duddingston Loch on a calm day.

Once the boat was safely berthed, Ann and I retired hurt. Chastened, but just glad to be alive. We abandoned all further thought of fishing and drove home; leaving Gladhouse trout unscathed, free to fight another day.

SKYE

HE Island of Skye, Eilean a Cheo, "island of mist", is one of Scotland's most popular tourist islands. Skye has everything for the perfect holiday: glorious scenery, attractive towns and villages, challenging mountains to climb, hill walking, fine beaches and charming people.

Visitors of Scottish descent from all over the world come to Skye to search for their clan roots. To Armadale Castle, home of Cloinne Domhnaill, "the family of Donald", Lords of the Isles and once the most powerful Highland clan; dramatic Dunvegan, ancient stronghold of Clan Macleod and still their home after 700 years.

From early April until late October, Skye bustles with activity and now that a bridge is proposed, linking Skye to mainland Scotland, I expect that the island will become even busier. I also suspect that Skye will lose some of its charm. That narrow strip of water, no matter how well served by ferries, was always a deterrent to casual visitors; once the bridge is built the old atmosphere, that sense of remoteness, may vanish.

I suppose that it is all a question of progress and priorities. Improved communications will undoubtedly stimulate commercial activity. But will the beauty and serenity of Skye disappear, submerged under the weight of unbridled tourism? Does more, necessarily mean better: visitors, income, industry, B & Bs, cafés, hotels and gift shops? I somehow doubt it.

Arriving on Skye the old way, by sea, is always special, a gesture of escapism, shrugging off twentieth-century shackles; a return to forgotten values. The island instantly embraces newcomers, enveloping them in a warm, comfortable blanket of peace and serenity. Arriving by bridge will never be the same.

In spite of all its attractions, Skye is not generally noted as a place to go for game fishing holidays. There are few rivers, and all Highland spate streams are dependent upon heavy rain to produce their best. Also, because of the mountainous nature of the terrain, there are few lochs; and reaching them involves more exercise than the average angler is prepared to expend. Which is excellent news for fishermen like me. A long, solitary walk to a distant loch, amidst glorious surroundings, is my ideal day out, regardless of size of fish or numbers caught. Skye meets these requirements in fullest measure, as well as offering a few more easily accessible venues for less adventurous spirits.

The best Skye brown trout water is Storr Loch, to the north of Portree. There used to be three separate lochs here: Leithan, Storr and Fada; but a small dam was built, thirty-six feet in height, across the principal inlet stream, linking them together. In reasonable water levels you can travel throughout the system, from one loch to another. At least you could the last time I was there.

A railway was built when the Storr Lochs were dammed; the only railway still in use on a Scottish island. A private line, the exclusive preserve of the engineer who looks after the power station at the foot of the sheer cliffs in Bearreraig Bay; and unlike mainland counterparts, Skye trains always run on time.

Fishing is managed by Portree Angling Association and they offer visiting anglers some really excellent sport at very modest cost, both from boat and bank.

The largest brown trout ever caught on Skye came from Storr and weighed 12lb, although the average weight of fish is a more modest 12oz.

Giving average weights can be dangerous. In my book, *The Trout Lochs of Scotland*, I remark that Storr fish weigh just under 1lb. I suppose it really depends upon conditions at the time, and I have had too many blank days to try and claim otherwise. Nevertheless, it does give anglers an indication of what they might expect to catch. The risk of doing so was demonstrated recently by a comment in the angling press. The writer, having fished Storr Lochs, suggested I should revise my average weight of fish, downwards, to 8oz. This drew a contradictory response from a Welsh angler who said that he and two friends fished Storr in 1985: "Taking the biggest wild brown trout of our quite lengthy fishing careers." Much to my relief.

There are few more splendid places to catch trout than in the shadow of the Trotternish Ridge. The Old Man of Storr dominates the horizon, a slim finger of rock guarding soft, green hills. Shapely Storr, the highest peak at 710 metres, leads northwards to Staffin and Quiraing; graced by The Ridge, Needle, Prison and The Table. Demanding climbing country.

Skye and climbing are synonymous, offering some of the most taxing rock climbs in Europe. The Needle on Quiraing was only conquered in August 1977, by Kevin Bridges, a young boy, sixteen-and-a-half years old. Mountaineer, W. A. Poucher, described the event:

> He began this very dangerous ascent by climbing a crack on its east face, above which he found the rock very fractured and loose. A traverse left and a groove led to a sound flake belay on the south-east arte, but his brother, Michael, who followed to this point considered it too risky to continue.
>
> Kevin climbed directly above the belay for some twenty-five feet and then traversed right to the north-east arte and continued to a grassy ledge, immediately below the summit. He placed four slings, linked together, round the top and abseiled down after leaving a small cairn there. Since the rock is so insecure he graded the climb as Very Severe.

Skye produces less dubious and dangerous pleasures, offering some delightful hill walks. Quarter of a mile west from Sligachan Hotel, a path leads southwards into Glen Brittle, climbing to the cairn at Bealach a' Mhaim. The view from Am Mam, north of the cairn, towards Cuillin, is magnificent.

An even more spectacular walk from Sligachan, is the route south through Glen Sligachan and Cuillin Hills to Loch Coruisk. A long, arduous tiring trek; but utterly rewarding, giving splendid views across Loch Scavaig, over Soay to the distant Island of Rhum.

The limestone outcrops at Storr and Trotternish nourish an astonishing array of wild flowers which make Skye a biologist's delight: Alpine Rock cress grows on high, rocky ledges; purple saxifrage can be found as early as March. May brings pink flowering campion, orchids, pipwort and mountain aven; followed by Guelder rose and helleborines.

Bird life is also of special interest, and hides have been erected in a number of places along the shores where you may watch a wide range of waders and divers: cuckoo arrive in June; moorlands and mountains host buzzard, merlin, peregrine and golden eagle; October brings whirring woodcock, grey-lag geese and snow-white Icelandic whooper swans.

With so much to do and see, there hardly seems to be enough time for fishing, but even at Trotternish there is much to interest the angler; a series of attractive hill lochs at the end of a long, hard walk, where the best fishing always is: Cleap, Corcasgil, Dubhar-Sgoth.

Once there, you are sure of absolute peace, and of catching your breakfast for the following day without too much difficulty. Another loch in this area, much more accessible, is Loch Mealt, and it contains a species of Arctic char which has remained virtually unchanged in character for thousands of years; probably since the last Ice Age.

Arctic char thrive in cold, deep waters and they inhabit many Scottish lochs. They never grow to great size, because their harsh habitat provides only a short summer feeding time; but they are lovely fish, distinguished by deeply forked tails and soft, blush-red sides.

In these remote, quiet places, there are often other creatures to be found round the shores of distant lochs and lochans, if you keep your eyes open. A movement in the grass could be a frog, or toad, or adder; but you rarely see them because they invariably see you first and slip quietly away.

But if you look carefully, particularly in summer months, during their breeding season, you may catch a glimpse of the rare Scottish newt. There are three species: common, crested and the palmate. And of course, the much larger, two-legged species, which is a lot easier to spot; generally late at night in northern towns, after closing time: the urban pi . . . d newt — but that's another story.

Other amphibians have been found in this area. One would have done credit to any glass case and measured ten feet in length, the largest amphibian found in the British Isles: a 70-million-year-old lizard. The creature is on display at Edinburgh's Queen Street Museum, in a very large glass case.

Salmon and sea-trout run most Skye streams and Portree Angling Association make much of this fishing available to visiting anglers. It is all a question of being in the right place at the right time. Usually during July and August, after heavy rain, fingers crossed, rod poised. After storms, rivers and burns can provide spectacular sport: Lealt, Brogaig, Kilmartin, Kilmluag, Conon, Rha. However, the best Skye salmon fishing is controlled by hotels.

Ullinish Lodge, built during the eighteenth century and visited by Dr Johnson and James Boswell in 1773, offers guests splendid sport on an estate that extends to some 27,500 acres; including fishing on Loch Duargrich, Ravaig and Conon, the whole of the river Ose and three miles of Upper Snizort.

Skeaboast House Hotel is an excellent Skye fishing hotel, standing in twelve acres of lovely gardens. Skeaboast boasts eight miles of both banks of the lovely Snizort River and when the water is high, guests experience salmon and sea-trout fishing that rivals anywhere in Scotland for quality.

The most famous mountains of Skye are the Cuillin Hills. They leap from the sea, a mighty symphony of dark rocks, a tangled, tortured mass, daring you to approach; and the finest way of doing so is by sea, watching these magical mountains slowly taking shape, growing in stature and magnificence.

The last time I visited Skye was by sea, as a crew-member of a thirty-nine-foot yacht. We sailed from Arduaine, south of Oban, inching our way carefully through the narrows between Fiola Meadhonach and Lunga; slipping past the Garvellach Isles as dawn blossomed.

As we left the shelter of Ross of Mull and passed the Holy Island of Iona, the engine was silenced and sails hoisted. So was I, unsuspectingly asleep after night watch.

The wind was north-easterly and I was berthed in a starboard bunk. As the vessel keeled over, cutting into the strong breeze, I was catapulted from my dreams, landing with a mighty thud on the galley table. Deeply shaken but wide awake.

116

We lunched in Gott Bay, Tiree, and spent the night at Arinagour on Coll. The following morning we headed north, past Muck, Eigg and the stark, sheer cliffs of Rhum, towards Cuilin and anchorage in the beautiful, green waters of Loch na Cuilce, at the head of Loch Scavaig.

It was late afternoon when we made landfall; but even then, the sun was dipping quickly behind Sgurr Alasdair, sending shafts of light glancing through the Cuilin Hills. We glided by Eilean Reamhar, lazy with curious seals, into the sheltered waters of Loch na Cuilce and dropped anchor.

The yacht was skippered by Peter Whitby and our party consisted of Peter's son and daughter, two of their friends, my elder brother, Ian, and his second son, James.

Before supper, we crowded ashore, climbing unsteadily up iron ladders to *terra firma* by the bothy overlooking the outlet stream from Loch Coruisk. English stone crop crouched in crevices weathered into slabs of dry rock; and the little river, sad in autumn drought, had barely enough force to reach the sea.

We scrambled to the top of Meall na Cuilce and looked down on Lady Coruisk, one of Scotland's most remote lochs; and one of the least known and yet most exciting sea-trout fisheries in the land, guarded by magnificent peaks: Sgurr Alasdair, Sgurr na Banachdich, Sgurr Ghreadaidh, Sgurr nan Gillean, and the long ridge of Druim nan Ramh.

The best account of sea-trout fishing on Loch Coruisk is contained in a marvellous book called *Fishing from Afar* by Stephen Johnson, published in 1947 by The University Press, Glasgow; now, sadly, out of print but still a game fishing classic. Johnson wrote the book whilst a POW in Germany during the last war.

He had been shot down in December 1942 and was incarcerated in Stalag Luft III, where he managed to acquire a notebook and pencil from Tim Fenn, the camp's Education Officer. To while away the long hours of imprisonment, Johnson wrote about his pre-war fishing holidays, many of which had been spent at Coruisk and Strathaird on Skye. The family used to travel to Strathaird in July and fish the tiny Kilmarie River, Camasunary River, Loch Creitheach and Loch Coruisk, often spending the night at the house by the shores of Camasunary Bay.

Johnson's account of his exploits, and the exploits of other members of his family, make fascinating reading. His father once took thirty sea-trout from Coruisk, weighing 40lb. Their best sea-trout, caught whilst trailing a salmon fly behind the boat, weighed 13lb 8oz.

Sea-trout are fidgety beasts, particularly when they have just arrived from feeding grounds. Their mouths are soft, and consequently, more are hooked and lost than hooked and caught. Their outstanding quality is the strength with which they fight and many anglers, including myself, consider sea-trout much more exciting fish to catch than salmon. Once hooked, sea-trout seem to run forever; and a big fish can have you down to the backing quicker than you can say Izaak Walton. Nor is there very much you can do to stop its mad rush, other than, if possible, run or row after it.

It is at moments like these that many an angler has regretted that hurriedly tied, bulky knot, joining backing to main line; as the fish disappears into the distance, sending the reel screaming, you suddenly remember. Will the ill-considered, bulky join pass through the rings of the rod? Why didn't you take more time? All one can do is hope and pray.

Stephen Johnson always advised friends to make sure they had plenty of backing for their reels, before fishing Coruisk; and he recounts the tale of one such guest preparing his tackle whilst travelling north by train, along the Highland Line, from Inverness to Kyle of Lochalsh.

Sorting out sixty yards of backing and joining it to thirty yards of casting line is serious business. I never attempt it alone, always waiting for some member of the family to wander by. I grab them, both their hands, and set about the task in spite of protests.

Johnson's friend had no such luck. Within minutes the inevitable tangles began to appear. First a minor, easily remedied knot, then more complicated bunches of line and backing. Believe me, very easily done. The more he pulled and tugged, the worse the mess grew and he struggled on until the whole thing was one unmitigated, tangled disaster.

This exhibition had been observed by the other occupants of the carriage; two ladies, heavily coated, prim-lipped and hatted, who watched without comment. They were busy knitting and the only sound in the carriage had been Johnson's friend's muted cursing and the clicking of their needles:

"He went along to the dining-car for lunch, leaving the whole thing in a dreadful tangle on the seat. He spent a long time over lunch as he dreaded facing the tangle again; but he needn't have worried. When he returned, the line and backing were neatly coiled in two separate heaps on the seat and the two old ladies were back at their knitting."

During his days at Strathaird, Johnson had marvellous sport. Even the tiny River Kilmarie produced some wonderful fish. There are two pools on the stream, Church Pool and Bridge Pool, from which Johnson once took a sea-trout of 4lb in weight.

Another notable basket of Coruisk sea-trout, caught at night, contained fifteen fish weighing 73lb; including eight fish of over 8lb and one of 9lb. It is unlikely that Coruisk will provide such outstanding sport today; off-shore netting has decimated sea-trout stocks and many of Scotland's finest sea-trout fisheries are but poor shadows of their former glory.

I stood at the mouth of the river, reluctant to return to the boat. In my mind's eye I saw Johnson and his friends, stalking their prey through the long, summer nights; saw the bend of the rod as a heavy fish "took"; heard again the mad scream of the reel and their cries of excitement. As I turned to go, a sea-trout leapt in the bay — a bar of purest silver, bright against the darkening sky.

The following morning we left Coruisk and sailed south with a following wind, past Elgol and the point of Sleat, to Mallaig, where we provisioned in the busy harbour. In the afternoon, warmed by glorious sunshine, we headed north through the Sound of Sleat.

On either side, mountains and hills lined the way. Past Armadale Castle, Knock Castle and Isleornsay on Skye; sailing grandly by the Rough Bounds of Knoydart, crowned by Sgurr na Ciche at the head of Loch Nevis, where Bonnie Prince Charlie hid from his pursuers in 1746 after the Battle of Culloden; and the wide jaws of Loch Hourn.

We had carefully timed our arrival at Kyle Rhea to coincide with floodtide, when the waters race through the narrows at great speed. To be more precise, Skipper Peter had done the timing. Being the least experienced member of the crew, I was deeply suspicious of the whole exercise; and even more so when I saw the turbulent stream. There were some anxious moments with the spinnaker as we jibbed, a lot of shouting and rope pulling, then we were flying, full-sailed before the wind, red-faced with pleasure, children cheering, at a speed approaching twelve knots.

That evening, we moored in a tiny anchorage across from Eilean Donan Castle, ancestral home of the Mackenzies of Kintail. King Haakon of Norway, on his way to defeat and disaster at the Battle of Largs in 1263 had rested nearby and the castle has a dramatic setting.

During the fifteenth and sixteenth centuries, Eilean Donan was the principal stronghold of the Mackenzies of Kintail and in 1719 it was held for the Jacobites by William Mackenzie, Earl of Seaforth, commanding a force of Spaniards. The castle was bombarded by three English ships and when the defending force surrendered, Eilean Donan was destroyed. The castle was restored in 1932 and today it is probably the most photographed of all Scottish keeps.

With sails tucked neatly away, we gathered in the cockpit and Peter congratulated his crew on their efforts during the race through Kyle Rhea: "Well done, everyone!" he exclaimed cheerfully. "We came through there like a well-oiled team." Still shaken, I grinned, and reaching for a large dram I replied: "Thank you, Peter, I don't mind if I do."

ST MARY'S LOCH

T MARY'S Loch in Ettrick Forest is a magical place where wizards and fairies still haunt the silent glens; peaceful and serene, surrounded by wild hills and distant moorlands, where curlew call and lark sing. The heartland of the Borders, peopled by a hardy and pragmatic race who have survived the slings and arrows of outrageous fortune for thousands of years.

Throughout history, the Scottish Borders have been both battleground and place of refuge; from Roman times, when Picts were ousted from their great fortress on Eildon Hill; William Wallace and Robert Bruce gained strength from this wilderness; King Henry IV passed this way when he burned the border abbeys in 1400; the tragedy of Flodden Field; the site of a hundred other personal fights and squabbles between rival border clans.

The only battles that rage now by St Mary's are between anglers and trout, and Tibbie Shiel's Inn, on the banks of St Mary's Loch, has been caring for travellers and fishermen for nearly 200 years.

The old hostelry, which dates from the late eighteenth century, is one of the most famous in the Scottish Borders. James Hogg, the Ettrick Shepherd, was a regular visitor, as was his friend, Sir Walter Scott. Another of Hogg's friends and drinking companions was Thomas Tod Stoddart, angler and author of the first book on Scottish fishing, *The Art of Angling as Practised in Scotland*, published in 1835 and later republished as *The Angler's Companion to the Rivers and Lakes of Scotland*.

Stoddart was trained as a lawyer, but throughout his life practised little other than fishing. He was stopped on the road once by the local magistrate who inquired what he was doing with himself these days. Outraged, Stoddart roared: "Doing man? Doing? I'm an angler."

Stoddart is best known for his life-long love affair with the River Tweed, and for his verses, of which my favourite is the "Angler's Complaint":

They've steekit the waters agen us, Jock,
　They've steekit the burnies an' a';
We hae na a chiel to befrien' us, Jock,
　Our laird's aye makin' the law.

We'll get neither yellow nor grey-fin, Jock,
　Nor bull-heid nor sawmon ava;
The laird he's aye at the savin', Jock,
　An' hauds to us weel wi' his law.

Yer flees ye may set them a-bleezin', Jock,
　Our wands they may gang to the wa';
It's neither in rhyme nor in reason, Jock,
　To coort a kick-up wi' the law.

That ilka intent should miscarry, Jock,
　I dinna wunner ava'
Our laird he's kin to the Shirra, Jock,
　And sib wi' the loons o' the law.

But faith, ye'll agree it's a hardship, Jock,
　To gie up our rights to the craw;
The neist time we meet wi' his lairdship, Jock,
　We promise him licks for his law.

An' e'en when the mirk is a-nearin', Jock,
　Wi' pock-nets and drag-nets an' a',
We'll gie his bit ponds sic a clearin', Jock,
　Our laird he'll look twice to the law.

We'll no spare a ged or a gudgeon, Jock,
　We'll no spare a fin or a jaw;
Lord pity the crazy curmudgeon, Jock,
　He'll sune tak his leave o' the law.

Stoddart and James Hogg were expert anglers and fished together many times on St Mary's Loch. One of their most notable days was 4 May 1833, when they shared a boat, catching seventy-nine trout weighing 36lb. No doubt they celebrated their victory over a dram or two with Tibbie.

Isobel, "Tibbie Shiels", the first owner of the inn, was born near Ettrick in 1783. In 1806 she married Robert Richardson who was employed as a mole-catcher on the Thirlestane Estate of Lord Napier. When her husband died suddenly in 1824, Tibbie was left almost destitute with a family of six children; so she decided to set up in business as an innkeeper to provide for her family.

Tibbie Shiel's Inn was much used by anglers who came to fish St Mary's Loch, but because of its association with James Hogg, Thomas Tod Stoddart, Sir Walter Scott, Robert Louis Stevenson, Thomas Carlyle and other literary figures, it soon became a gathering place for poets, writers and journalists as well. In his excellent booklet, *Tibbie Shiels*, published in 1986, Michael Robson recounts an early visitor's impressions of the inn:

> The old fashioned kitchen of Tibbie Shiel's Inn was the model of what a kitchen ought to be; it had such an air of cosy warmth and welcoming hospitality. In the vast open fireplace were glowing peat embers, the kettle sang on the hob, the white-faced grandfather's clock ticked beside the 'bink', and was there ever anything so quaintly picturesque as the box beds with their sliding doors? But best of all was Tibbie's spinning-wheel on one side of the hearth, and Sir Walter Scott's armchair on the other.

Another patron of Tibbie's, and friend of the group, was Christopher North, pen name of Professor John Wilson, lawyer and Professor of Moral Philosophy at Edinburgh University in 1820. Wilson described Tibbie as being "a shrewd, kindly, comely woman" and, given Wilson's reputation, Tibbie must have had a strong personality to keep her distinguished guests in order. His friend, William Maguire, wrote of him as: "A sixteen stoner — a cocker, a racer, a six-bottler, a twenty-four tumbler — an out and outer — a true upright, knocking-down, poetical, prosaic, moral, professional, hard-drinking, fierce-eating, good-looking honourable, and straight-forward Tory."

John Wilson was a well-known sportsman and keen angler. He bestowed upon himself such titles as MA, Master of Angling, and FRS, Fisherman Royal of Scotland; but he is best remembered for his column in *Blackwoods Magazine*. The articles were written under his pen name "Christopher North" and describe the adventures and exploits of North and the Shepherd, who was James Hogg, and Tickler, John Gibson Lockhart, who married Sophia, Sir Walter Scott's elder daughter. Lockhart was described by Hogg as: "A mischievous Oxford puppy for whom I was terrified; dancing after the young ladies and drawing caricatures of everyone who came in contact with him."

North's *Noctes Ambrosiane* and later *Recreations of Christopher North* lampooned polite Edinburgh society and were instantly popular. They included frequent references to the great angling exploits of the Shepherd, as in *Splendide Mendax*, when Hogg "tops" one of North's fishing tales:

> *Shepherd*: Poo, that was nae day's fishin' ava, man, in comparison to ane o' mine on St Mary's Loch. To say naething about the countless sma' anes, twa hunder about half a pun', ae hunder about a haill pun', fifty about twa pun', five-and-twenty about fowre pun', and the lave rinnin' frae half a stane up to a stane and a half, except about half a dizzen, aboon a' weicht that put Geordie Gudefallow and Huntly Gordon to their mettle to carry them pechin to Mount Benger on a haun-barrow.

It was rumoured that Tibbie Shiels had a "soft spot" for James Hogg and towards the end of her life she is reported as saying: "Yon Hogg, the Shepherd, ye ken, was an awfu' fine man. He should hae tae'n me, for he cam coortin' for years, but he just gaed away and took another."

Tibbie outlived most of her more famous customers and died in July 1878 at the age of ninety-six; but the memory of the charm of the innkeeper by St Mary's Loch and her famous customers lives on. Tibbie Shiels is a place of pilgrimage to this day.

I was first introduced to James Hogg in the Lyceum Theatre, Edinburgh, during the International Festival, when Ann and I attended a stage production of his novel, *The True Confession of a*

124

Justified Sinner. There was a lot of shouting and running about, dramatic gestures and sparse, unworldly scenery, so I nudged Ann, and we slipped quietly from the theatre, down the street to the nearest pub, leaving the justified sinner to get on with his confession in peace. Or, more accurately, as it seemed to me, unbridled fury.

James Hogg, the Ettrick Shepherd, was born in 1770 and he described his great novel as a revelation that "salvation was not contingent upon faith, but was the effect of justification, of grace". I still find the book hard to understand, but readily acknowledge its stature as one of the most significant works of Scottish literature.

Hogg's poetry, however, is another matter and in it, I believe, he sometimes rivals Burns and frequently surpasses Sir Walter Scott, his friend and mentor:

> See yonder pawkie shepherd,
>   That lingers on the hill,
> His ewes are in the fauld,
>   An' his lambs are lying still;
> Yet he dawna gang to bed,
>   For his heart is in a flame,
> To meet his bonny lassie
>   When the kye comes hame.

Hogg was a border shepherd, born at Ramsaycleuch in the Ettrick Forest, son of an impoverished farmer. He had little formal education, certainly no more than a year, and confessed that even at the age of twenty he had difficulty reading and writing.

Like Robert Burns, Hogg was influenced by his family and surroundings. His parents were deeply religious and much given to long, scriptural arguments. Their stern Calvinistic faith was nurtured by one of the Borders most famous preachers, Thomas Boston. People would walk miles each Sunday to hear Boston preach and his congregation generally numbered upwards of 700 thirsting souls.

Hogg's grandfather, known as "Will o' the Phaup", was reputed to have conversed with the fairies, and Hogg liked to refer to himself as "King of the Mountain Fairy School" of poets. The songs he composed for local girls brought him great popularity, but throughout his life, as poet, writer and novelist, Hogg never achieved the recognition his work deserved, in spite of constant support and encouragement from Scott.

Hogg and Sir Walter Scott were introduced to each other in 1802, by John Leyden, another shepherd's son and poet, when Scott was collecting stories and tales for his *Border Minstrelsy*. James Hogg's mother was well known in the area as a positive mine of such information, and the two men struck up a friendship that lasted all their lives. Hogg said Scott was: "the best and most steady friend I ever had to depend on". Hogg's mother was not so certain about Sir Walter, or his inquisitiveness concerning traditional Border ballads, and she is reported to have told the great man, crossly: "They were made for singin' and no' for reading; but ye hae broken the charm an' noo they'll niver be sung mair."

Scott's namesake, Michael Scott, might have agreed. He was known as "Scott the Wizard" and Sir Walter claimed him as an ancestor. The Wizard was born in 1175 and after an extensive education, at Oxford, Paris and Bologna in Italy, lived most of his life in the Borders. He is reputed to have set a devil to work, to keep him from harming the local community. The devil's first task was splitting the Eildon Hills into three parts, then constructing a stone dam across the River Tweed. The final task, which kept the devilish intruder busy for ever, was to weave a rope, out of sand. The "wondrous wizard's" grave may still be seen to this day at Melrose Abbey.

During the latter years of the eighteenth century this small corner of the Borders was home to a remarkable number of outstanding men. John Leyden, born at Denholm on 8 September 1775, was a poet and Orientalist of international fame. After graduating from St Andrews University, Leyden took up a medical appointment in Madras, India, and translated the bible into several far eastern languages. He died in Java on 28 August, 1811.

Mungo Park, the explorer, another farmer's son, was born at Foulshiels, on 20 September, 1771, near the "Meeting of the Waters", where the rivers Ettrick and Yarrow mingle; and as a surgeon, he joined the East India Company in 1792. Three years later he was employed by the African Association to explore the River Niger, which he followed almost to Timbuktu. Park's book of his journey, *Travels in the Interior Districts of Africa, Performed in the years 1795, 1796 and 1797* is a masterpiece of its kind and

Thomas Carlyle described Park as being: "one of the most unpretending and at the same time valuable specimens of humanity".

But no man is ever a hero in his own home, and the story is told of Mungo returning from one of his expeditions to his parents' house. When the explorer knocked on the door, late one evening, his mother inquired: "Who in the world could that be?" One of Park's brothers is reputed to have replied: "Oh, that will be oor Mungie. I saw him at the market the day."

After a short period as a doctor in Peebles, in 1805 Park set out once more for Africa, along with his brother-in-law, Thomas Anderson, and forty-five British soldiers and a large contingent of native porters. The expedition ended in disaster. After a canoe journey of some 1,000 miles, Park and his companions were attacked by natives at Yuri. During the fight their vessel capsized and they drowned. Of the party that had set out with such high hopes from Pisania in Gambia, only three soldiers and one native bearer survived to tell the sad tale.

But perhaps the most famous Border man was Walter Scott, born in Edinburgh in 1771 where his father was a lawyer. His mother, Anne Rutherford, was the daughter of Dr John Rutherford, Professor of Medicine at Edinburgh University; and both parents were descended from ancient Border families: the Scotts of Harden and Buccleuch, and, on his mother's side, the Swintons.

Scott's early years were spent at his grandfather's farm at Sandyknowe, near the old Border tower of Smailholm. An attack of poliomyelitis as a child left Scott lame for life, but nevertheless, he was a tall, strong man, noted for his outdoor and sporting interests.

Smailholm must have greatly influenced the young Scott. The gaunt, dramatic tower stands on a rock ledge, 700 feet high, dominating the surrounding landscape. Similar Pele Towers are scattered throughout the Borders, watch-towers and forts against the incursions of raiders from across the border.

The disaster of Flodden Field in September 1513, when the flower of Scotland fell around their impetuous king, James IV, prompted the building of these towers. An Act of Parliament in 1535 ordered that any man owning land worth more than £100 should build a Pele Tower for the protection of his dependants;

and even as late as 1804, fires were placed on the towers to warn of approaching danger, should Napoleon succeed in his plans to invade Britain.

Scott is, in my opinion, the outstanding figure of Scottish literature; and I first met Sir Walter, and his work, at the Royal High School of Edinburgh, where Scott was a pupil. A bust of Sir Walter sat on a window-ledge at the bottom of a flight of stairs leading to the English department, and each year, with irreverent glee, we used to give our famous former pupil a red nose.

In time, I learned to love Scott and, in doing so, simply followed a long-established tradition; because Scott was as much admired for his qualities as a man as he was for his excellence as a writer. Byron, in the midst of public scandal, wrote to his friend Scott: "I owe you far more than the usual obligation for the courtesies of literature, for you went out of your way in 1817 to do me a service when it required not merely kindness, but courage to do so"; and he said that Scott was "as nearly a thorough good man as a man can be".

The sheer volume of work Scott produced, let alone its quality, leaves anyone who pretends to be a writer aghast. Often, when struggling with words before my high-tech word-processing system, I think of the great man, in his dark little study at Abbotsford, scratching away with pen and ink, hour after hour, and yet still finding time to be the most devoted of husbands and caring of fathers.

Abbotsford, Scott's magnificent home overlooking the sweetly flowing Tweed, was purchased in 1811 and named after a crossing place on the river used by the monks from Melrose Abbey. When financial disaster overtook him because of his interest in Ballantyne's publishing business, Scott's creditors gave him the house; and it has remained in the family ever since.

Like most of his contemporaries, Scott was a great traveller and at times I think that the rough roads of Scotland must have been positively jammed with artists and literati, notebooks poised, tramping their way round the country. Caustic Welshman, Thomas Pennant; Johnson and Boswell; Wordsworth, and sister Dorothy; Robert Burns; Mrs Murray; Samuel Taylor Coleridge; Southey and Thomas Telford; Queen Victoria and Prince Albert; Baden Powell; and many more. Battalions of them, all describing and commenting upon what they saw.

James Hogg also went "walk-about", writing regular reports of his travels to Sir Walter Scott, who persuaded the editor of the *Scots Magazine* to publish them as a series of articles which appeared in that magazine from 1802 until 1804.

Hogg tramped many weary miles, faithfully recording his impressions along the way, and his account tells as much about the writer as it does about what he reports of the countryside. His personal diary reveals a kind, thoughtful, decent man, with a wonderful sense of humour, courteous and friendly at all times and in all circumstances.

In 1802, Hogg travelled from Etterick (Hogg's spelling), by way of Edinburgh to Perth, then on to Blair-in-Athol and Dalnacardoch. The following year he toured the Highlands, leaving home on 27 May and arriving in the Trossachs on 29 May; visiting Rob Roy's home at Glen Gyle by Loch Katrine, and Inveraray Castle on Wednesday, 1 June. From Inveraray, Hogg went north, to Fort William, Lochaber, Kinlochewe and Dundonnel; and then over the Minch to the Outer Hebrides and the "heather isle" of Lewis.

Hogg's last tour in 1804, took him, mostly by sea, to Argyllshire, the Braes of Ardnamurchan and back to the Outer Hebrides. He was so enraptured with the island of Harris that he considered moving there permanently. But the journey almost cost him his life when their vessel, the *Johnson*, "a strong, English-built sloop", was nearly wrecked in Loch Sunart in a mighty gale, vividly described by Hogg in his letters.

James Hogg was a happy man who enjoyed his hard, active life, saying that he couldn't "distinguish one part from another, save by some remarkably good day's fishing".

St Mary's Loch still keeps anglers happy and content and although the great days of Hogg, Stoddart and Wilson have long since gone, good catches are often taken. Brown trout average approximately 10oz in weight and most seasons produce a few fish of over 3lb. As always, it is all a matter of being in the right place at the right time, with the correct fingers crossed.

West of Tibbie Shiel's Inn is a statue of Hogg, holding his shepherd's crook, stone-deep in thought, watching rising trout he may no longer catch, hearing new voices telling old stories of ones that got away. In his hand is a scroll inscribed with words from his poem, "The Queen's Wake": "He taught the wandering winds to sing."

And in the bar, the ghosts of the literary 'old boys' of the loch gather round: Thomas Stoddart, choosing a fly; Lochart, eyeing a pretty barmaid; John Wilson, warming himself for the fray with a large dram; Sir Walter, nodding by the fireplace; all still kept in good order and splendid discipline by the shades of Tibbie, one of the Borders most enduring and best-loved characters.

LOMOND

OCH Lomond is Scotland's best-known and best-loved loch, famous throughout the world. The sad lyric and haunting melody of the song "The Bonnie Banks o' Loch Lomon' " echo down the ages, etched on the heart of all those who call Scotland home.

The origin of both words and music is unknown, but tradition has it that the song was written by a Jacobite prisoner the night before his execution in Carlisle, during the disastrous 1745 Rebellion, bidding farewell to his wife as she starts her solitary journey back to Scotland. There is a Celtic belief that when a Scot dies in a foreign land, his soul travels home by the "low road" and the doomed man was comforted by this thought as he awaited the hangman's noose: "O, you'll tak' the high road, and I'll tak' the low road, and I'll be in Scotland afore ye; but me and my true love will never meet again, on the bonnie, bonnie banks o' Loch Lomon'."

Today, the bonnie banks are more busy, but those who meet there now, still have their heads firmly attached to their shoulders. Unlike Jacobite ghosts who paid the ultimate price for their support of Charles Edward Stewart, the Young Pretender to Britain's throne.

Most visitors catch their first glimpse of the loch from the A82, an incredibly busy, tortuous road that winds up the western shore from Alexandria to Ardlui. I did, many years ago, and then, as now, road works blocked our way. Indeed, it seems to me that improvements to the A82 have been in progress since Noah's Flood, and are likely to continue until the end of time.

The eastern shore, from Balmaha north to Inversnaid, used to be much quieter. Past Rowardennan, access was by foot and screaming hoards were quickly left behind. Now, with the building of the long-distance footpath, the West Highland Way, even this once-remote land bustles with hikers and campers.

The route extends ninety-five miles, from Mullguy, sorry Milngavie, just north of Glasgow, to Fort William, at the southern end of the Great Glen. The Rowardennan to Inverarnan section is very popular, cluttered with direction poles, markers, signposts, bridges and other artificial structures, all deemed essential by planners.

I fail to understand why authority and officialdom feel compelled to designate rural routes and paths. If people wish to explore Scotland they are perfectly at liberty to do so. There is no need to lay out rustic 'motorways', which soon become as jammed with travellers as their urban counterparts. This section of the Way is notoriously muddy and has suffered dreadfully from erosion, caused by thousands of tramping feet.

Perhaps it has something to do with job creation. Or, more probably, job justification. The more nonsensical, costly, unnecessary schemes chair-bound officials can dream up, then the longer their sinecures may last. The tragedy is, however, that many of these plans seem to speed up the destruction of that which they purport to preserve.

In spite of being within easy reach of half the population of Scotland, and being a magnet for thousands of tourists, 40,000 of whom may be found round the loch on a warm summer day, Loch Lomond still manages to retain its special charm; and with a little effort it is generally possible to find a private corner, away from the madding crowd.

Other local residents, midges, are far more madding and difficult to avoid. The ferocity of Lomond midges defies description; and I speak as someone who has suffered the stings and needle-like barbs of this outrageous clan from Sutherland to Solway — Lomond midges can clear a picnic-site quicker than a Free Kirk minister in full flood.

There are thirty-four known species of bloodsucking insects in

Scotland and one innocent-looking acre of moorland can contain up to ten million midge larvae. Not surprisingly, a recent book on *culoicides impunctatus* by George Hendry was a best-seller in Scotland. In it, Hendry describes, with almost reverential regard, how the midge attacks: "If a landing is successful the midge will wander over the surface of the skin, presumably searching for a suitable soft area before beginning the task of cutting into the epidermis. If the midge continues to escape unwelcome attention, some three to four minutes will be spent feeding on blood."

I have long since resigned myself to the fact that midges are part of Scottish life. A small price to pay for my enjoyment and pleasure of the countryside. After all, we each have about 5.6 litres of blood. Why be parsimonious? But I freely confess that a warm summer evening by the bonnie banks strains even my resolve, mightily.

One place on Loch Lomond where I have never been troubled by midges is the lovely island of Inchmurrin, the Island of Hospitality, and it may be argued that this location, more than any other, offers an open invitation for mass attacks.

Scotland's oldest naturist organisation, The Scottish Outdoor Club, which celebrated its fiftieth anniversary in 1988, has a site on the island; and when my wife Ann and I visited Inchmurrin a few years ago, in spite of warm weather, midges were noticeable by their absence. Along with our youngest daughter, Jean, we hired a boat from Balmaha and sailed south-west past Inchcailloch and Ross Priory, arriving at the club mooring-bay forty-five minutes later.

The weather was superb and we were made most welcome by the members; lazing away a few happy days at peace with the world, returning refreshed, relaxed, and all-over-tanned. Few human joys can match the wonderful pleasure of feeling God's hot sun warming ones body; or the silky, all-enveloping embrace of cool loch water, soothing the soul.

Inchmurrin owes its name to St Mirren, patron saint of Paisley, and the island was once a home to the Earls of Lennox. Their ruined castle may still be visited, and it was here that Isabella, Duchess of Albany, fled after James I removed the heads of most of her relatives, in 1425, at Stirling Castle.

In an attempt to thwart the ambitions of Duke Murdoch, head of the Albany Stewarts, separated from absolute power by only the dying king and his twelve-year-old son, Robert III of Scotland decided to send the future James I to France, for his own safety. A chapter of suspicious 'accidents' delayed James's departure from the Bass Rock in the Firth of Forth, and by the time the vessel, the *Maryenknygt*, set sail, news of King Robert's plan had somehow reached the sharp ears of King Henry IV of England.

The *Maryenknygt* was intercepted off Flamborough Head on 14 March 1406 and James found himself incarcerated in the Tower of London. When King Robert died, three weeks later, Albany became Governor and virtual king of Scotland in all but name; and during his period of office, he did little to secure James's release.

After eighteen years, James returned to Scotland to claim his inheritance, arriving at Melrose on 4 April 1424. The time of reckoning was at hand for the Albany Stewarts. On 24 May 1425, Walter Stewart, the Duke's eldest son, was beheaded. Duke Murdoch and his son, Alexander, and the Earl of Lennox, followed their kinsman to the block the next day. The power of the Albany Stewarts was broken and their lands forfeited, including Inchmurrin Castle, which surrendered to King James on 8 June 1425.

Many of my own Lomond battles started from St Mirren's town of Paisley, in company with the late Charles Hodget, a local businessman, and a friend of mine, Tony Sykes, from Bridge of Weir. Both keen fishermen.

I once met them at Glasgow Airport on their return from an Irish angling holiday. Both looked the worse for wear and lumbered towards me, hands outstretched, staggering from side to side. "Good Lord," I exclaimed. "What's wrong with your legs?" They were still wearing their waders. Not only because that was the best way to carry them, but also because they had been fishing until the last moment; taking down their rods whilst sprinting across the tarmac to the waiting aircraft.

Only one thing used to delay their arrival at loch or river: the necessity for pre-fishing refreshment along the way. A fact I discovered, much to my cost, the first time they invited me to join them for a day's fishing on Lomond.

After several "pit-stops" we eventually reached Balmaha, launched our boat, and set off towards the islands, where salmon lie. Or should.

134

Fingers crossed, light of battle glinting in my eyes, anticipation high, I quietly thanked my hosts for inviting me; but as Charles set the boat for a drift down the south shore of Inchcruin, I discovered why I had been included in the party: "Now, Bruce, you sit in the middle with the dapping-rod. Keep the fly dancing on the surface. When you see a salmon making towards it, lift the fly off the water," he explained. "What will you and Tony be doing?" I inquired suspiciously. "Tony will fish from the bow, I'll be in the stern. You see, when the dap is removed, the salmon turn and take on of our flies. Got it?" I had, and did, for several hours.

Which gave me plenty of time to ponder a Scottish geographical and historical quirk which has always fascinated me.

Until the thirteenth century, Loch Lomond was known as Loch Leven, after the name of the river which drains it into the Firth of Clyde; and guarding the loch is Ben Lomond, Scotland's southernmost Munro. On the other side of Scotland, another hill and another loch have the same names: Loch Leven in Kinross, Scotland's most famous brown trout water, drained by its River Leven into the Firth of Forth, guarded by West Lomond; not so majestic as its western namesake, but just as lovely in its own right.

The link is the word "lomond", which is derived, or is supposed to be derived, from the old British word, "lumin" meaning beacon: in Gaelic, "Beinn Iaomainn" mountain of the beacon.

In days past, our ancestors, the Picts, "the painted men", presumably used the Lomonds as watch-towers. Peering south through the mist, as Roman legions, steel kilts clanking through the forests, brought the dubious benefits of civilisation north, a beacon was lit to warn the tribes of approaching danger.

The Romans never succeeded in subduing Scotland, in spite of their best efforts. Later invading hordes, Angles, Saxons, Jutes, Vikings, English, were equally unsuccessful. It was left to the Scots themselves to give up their birthright and freedom, in 1707, when Scottish lords and lairds sold their country and its people for a few handfuls of English gold.

A handful of silver splashed in the water by the boat, as a salmon rose to the dapping fly. I felt a single, great tug, and the fish was gone. My companions turned on me with fury: "You didn't remove the dap, Bruce. What are you thinking of. Pay attention, for goodness sake."

"Thirsty work this, you know chaps. Perhaps a small warmer

would help me concentrate. What do you think?" Like lightning, two hip flasks were produced and proffered. "How very kind," I said. "I should be able to concentrate for at least another ten minutes, before I get thirsty again."

Loch Lomond and the River Leven are excellent salmon and sea-trout fisheries; and many of the surrounding feeder streams can be just as productive, particularly the River Endrick, flowing swiftly from the Fintry Hills through fine, fertile lands to lady Lomond.

Two books tell you all you need to know about fishing on Lomond: Ian Wood's *Loch Lomond* and Bill McEwan's *Angling on Lomond*. These works are recognised classics, written by two of the most respected anglers in Scotland, both now sadly fishing that "great loch in the sky"; much missed and fondly remembered by their many friends.

I had read both books, very carefully, before setting out, but fishing is a funny thing, where nothing is certain, nothing ever assured. We fished hard all day, and if we had caught just two more fish, we would have had a brace between us for our efforts.

Other anglers are more lucky. When I catch fish, it is skilful, when my companions do so, I refer to it as luck; and I once got into serious trouble because of this claim.

Not really my fault. A Midlands angler was holding forth in the bar one night (I'm sure you have met the type), at great, boring length, about salmon fishing in general, and his skill, knowledge and excellence in catching them in particular. Exasperated, I interrupted: "Really, if you will excuse me saying, that is nonsense. Every true angler knows ninety-five per cent of all fish caught are caught by luck." It quickly became apparent that this fishing paragon was quite unused to being stopped in mid-flow. He was silent for a moment, then a sly smile spread slowly over his face.

"All right then, smart Alec, if you know so much about it, tell me this: how are the other five per cent caught?" Savouring the moment, I replied, "Skill, obviously. Those are the fish I catch." He went bright scarlet, fists clenched, and had to be restrained from assault and battery.

But really, fishing is not a science, to be academicised; nor is it a competitive sport, like football or rugby, where spectators scream for blood, although commercial interests are trying to turn it into that. No, fishing is a gentle art, an individual treasure, given to man by the gods, for personal pleasure, comfort and enjoyment. It always has been, and always will be.

To protect the beauty of Loch Lomond and its outstanding environmental richness, much of the area has been designated as a Site of Special Scientific Interest by the Nature Conservancy Council, the government's environmental "watch-dog".

The N.C.C. is under almost constant attack from land-owning and commerical interests, who wish to exploit the environment for private profit; and I firmly believe that were it not for the activities of the N.C.C., Scotland's greatest asset, its landscape and natural beauty, would soon disappear.

Already, we have seen blanket afforestation destroy much of the Flow Country of Caithness and East Sutherland; vast quarries scar once magnificent hills; unsightly electricity pylons stride over glen and moorland like giant creatures from outer space; reservoirs, hydroelectric schemes and fish farms mar the landscape. The N.C.C. should be supported, in all its efforts, and the present proposals to split the N.C.C. into three separate bodies, covering England, Wales and Scotland is, in my opinion, nothing other than an attempt to emasculate environmental concern. The plan should be resisted by all who love Scotland's countryside.

There are seventeen different species of fish in Loch Lomond, including salmon, sea-trout, brown trout, powan, stickleback, some huge pike and three different species of lamprey; and of these, the powan, a member of the salmon family, is most threatened.

Powan are quite unique. Only found in Scotland in Loch Lomond and nearby Loch Eck, which drains into the Holy Loch through the River Eachaig, concern has been expressed recently about their status and survival prospects.

Powan are known as the freshwater herring, and resemble herring in size and also in their high, protein-packed food value. How many still exist in Lomond and Eck is uncertain, because they are secretive fish which tend to live at great depth, so you don't often see them. But during the last war, something like 200,000 powan were netted out of Loch Lomond each year to help feed Glasgow. Now, a research programme has been instigated to examine the present status of powan in both lochs, and the future for this sparkling little fish looks brighter than it has done for decades.

Bright prospects can also be seen from the summit of Ben Lomond, probably Scotland's most-climbed mountain, visited by upwards of 3,000 walkers and climbers each year. The most popular route is from the carpark at Rowardennan and the ascent takes about three-and-a-half hours, depending upon how often you stop to admire the view along the way. From the top, on a clear day, half of Scotland lies before you, from Merrick in the south to Ben More and Ben Nevis northwards. Below, the shining waters of the island-scattered loch, and beyond, the Arrochar Alps and Inner Hebridean isles: Jura, Kintyre and Arran.

The beauty of Loch Lomond has attracted some very famous visitors, including Scotia's bard, Robert Burns, on his second northern tour, in 1787, when he describes a mad horse-race he had, down the banks of Loch Lomond, against a Highlander, riding without stirrups.

William Wordsworth and his sister Dorothy, the inevitable sister Dorothy, trekked by Loch Lomond to the Trossachs, the bristling country, in company with the poet Samuel Taylor Coleridge, who seems to me to have been a gloomy sort of companion to have along on such a glorious journey.

They stayed at Luss, and crossed from there to Inversnaid, on the east shore, where Wordsworth noticed the lass of his famous poem, "Highland Girl" the daughter of the ferryman: "Sweet Highland Girl, a very shower of beauty is thy earthly dower." And later, another highland lass he immortalized in the lovely poem, "The Solitary Reaper": "Behold her single in the field, yon solitary Highland Lass, reaping and singing by herself, stop here or gently pass." Had his good moments, Wordsworth. And an eye for the lassies.

Nor would any description of walking in Scotland be complete without mention of Johnson and his lapdog, Boswell. Boswell records that the pair, who invented the concept of "free-loading", stayed at the house of Sir James Colquhoun, visiting the islands on the loch, and then by the River Leven with Mr Smollet, a relation of Dr Smollet: "The civility and respect which we found at every place, it is ungrateful to omit, and tedious to repeat."

Near by, another great Scottish hero, King Robert I, had a palace at Cardross, to the west of Dumbarton, and he eventually died there, of leprosy, comforted it is said, by his second wife and his falcon.

Of less comfort to Scotland's monarchs were Clan Gregor, who claimed much of these lands as their own. Their exploits involved the removal of anything that wasn't securely nailed down, and to subdue the clan, during the eighteenth century, the government built a fort at Inversnaid, on the shores of Loch Lomond. The Macgregors attacked and burned it to the ground, disarming the soldiers; as soon as Inversnaid was rebuilt, the Macgregors, led by Rob Roy's nephew, attacked again and destroyed the fort.

Inversnaid was rebuilt, for the third time, and on this occasion the commander was none other than the soldier Wolfe, who refused to shoot a wounded Highlander after the Battle of Culloden when commanded to do so by Butcher Cumberland, offering his resignation instead.

Wolfe set about the task with his customary efficiency, sending regular reports to his superior, General Bland, at Stirling Castle; but Wolfe never liked either Scotland or its inhabitants, claiming that they were, "better governed by fear than favour".

Another famous visitor to Loch Lomond was Sir Walter Scott, whilst researching his book on Rob Roy. When Scott arrived at Inversnaid, he found the old garrison gone, the fort locked and a single retired pensioner in charge, working a sparse crop of barley. Sir Walter asked to look round the fort and was told that the key was under a stone by the door.

Scott entered the fort with a lot less trouble than the man he was studying. Rob Roy had little use for keys and preferred more robust methods of gaining entry. Sir Walter mused a space amongst the Grey ruins. No doubt dashing off a few chapters whilst so doing.

And as the great man walked home, perhaps he rehearsed a few lines from the old song:

> 'Twas there that we parted in yon shady glen,
>   On the steep, steep sides of Ben Lomon',
> Where in purple hue the hieland hills we view,
>   An' the moon coming out in the gloamin'.

LOCH LEVEN

N O ONE specifically told me Loch Leven was special. I just seemed to know. As a child knows its parents are the most important people in its life. Scottish anglers are born nurturing a similar, deeply rooted reverence for Loch Leven, and to visit Scotland without casting a fly on this world-famous water would be little other than criminal angling negligence.

The quality of Loch Leven trout is legendary; remarkably beautiful fish, silver in colour, dark-spotted and perfectly shaped. Their flesh is salmon-pink, nourished by millions of freshwater shrimps and *daphnia* that abound in the lime-rich water, and mature, larger fish, have a golden, yellow tinge to their underside, which in old days gave them the nickname, "yellow-bellies".

The largest trout taken from Leven was caught on 8 September, 1911, by a Colonel Scott and it weighed 9lb 13oz. A number of other excellent trout have been caught over the years, including W. Hatten's 6lb 3oz fish in 1980, Eugune Grube's 5lb 12oz fish in 1983, and in August 1989, a trout weighing 6lb 6oz, caught by Cowdenbeath angler, Francis Jarrett; but fish of more than 3lb are the exception rather than the rule, and the average weight of trout is in the order of 1lb 1oz.

Most seasons, upwards of 25,000 fish are caught — although this figure used to be considered low in the glory-days of the loch, between the wars and during the 1950s and early 1960s. The 1929 season produced more than 50,000 trout; in 1960, the last cyclical peak, some 80,000 fish were caught.

Since then catches have fallen drastically, in some years to below 10,000, and in 1984 Sir David Montgomery, who owns Loch Leven, announced a restocking programme designed to introduce 70,000 new fish to supplement existing stock. A similar exercise was carried out in the 1930s, when Loch Leven was leased to P. D. Malloch, of the Perth angling family, when thousands of fish were reared in ponds along the north shore and released into the loch. After several seasons the practice was discontinued when it failed to materially effect catches; and it has been suggested that the present programme will have as little effect.

The real problem facing Scotland's premier trout fishery is not lack of numbers, but rather a change in trout feeding habits. Intensive farming practices round the shores have massively increased pollution: sewage, industrial waste, insecticides, chemicals, leading to near-eutrophication. Fishing Leven in the mid-1960s was, at times, like fishing pea-green soup.

I remember one day, fishing with a friend, Tony Sykes, and his father, Charles, from Bridge of Weir near Glasgow. Mr Sykes senior, our kind host, was a meticulous man, who did not suffer fools gladly, and insisted that "things" should be done "properly". After a couple of fishless drifts, he laid down his rod, produced a large hip flask and poured three good drams. Dipping a cup into the pea-soup, Charles splashed it liberally into the whiskies: "Here you are, chaps, nothing like a taste of good old Loch Leven water to help make fish rise. Cheers." Downed in a single gulp.

Tony and I were more circumspect and, in order not to give offence, emptied our glasses into the loch when Father Sykes was busy looking the other way. Hours later, at dinner that night, Charles Sykes turned to me and inquired, nonchalantly, but with a faintly troubled look in his eyes: "How is the quality of Loch Leven water these days, Bruce?" You should know, I thought to myself, considering how much of it you drank this afternoon. "Has been better, Mr Sykes. Too much fertiliser and raw sewage for my liking," I replied truthfully. "Really?" Charles Sykes went pale. "If you will excuse me, I think I'll go to bed now. You pair fish on tomorrow, I have to get back to Glasgow, urgently."

In such sad water conditions, there are few surface hatches of fly and consequently trout tend to root about the bottom, picking up food well below the surface, rarely rising naturally. In times past, a hatch of flies on Loch Leven was a marvellous sight to behold with thousands of insects dancing across the waves on gossamer wings, pursued by eagerly feeding trout. Then, as far as the eye could see, the surface was alive with rising fish. Huge fins, like great sails, gliding by the boat, arrowing unerringly towards their prey. Sport was fast and furious. Never, before or since, have I had such fine fishing, or caught finer fish.

Since the 1850s, Loch Leven trout have been exported throughout the world. When Britannia ruled the waves, the administrators of our far-flung domains introduced Loch Leven trout to native waters to provide relaxation from arduous colonial duties: India, Africa, Australia, New Zealand, North America, Argentina and the Falkland Islands, where Leven trout reverted to sea-feeding, becoming, to all intents and purposes, superb, hard-fighting sea-trout.

Loch Leven used to contain sea-trout and salmon. After the last Ice Age, when retreating ice formed the loch and the River Leven connected it to the Firth of Forth, migratory fish would run the system, to spawn in the burns feeding Loch Leven; so some of the present stock of fish still probably have a sea-going, genetic implant, waiting to be activated by the first whiff of salt.

Up until 1830, the loch was considerably larger than it is today, being some four miles long by three miles wide. Indeed, water lapped at the foot of the tower on Castle Island, where Mary, Queen of Scots, languished after the Battle of Carberry; and there were only four, not seven, islands visible: St Serf's, Castle Island, Reed Bower, Roy's Folly.

In 1830, a drainage scheme was completed to improve surrounding agricultural land, and the level of the loch fell by more than five feet in consequence, reducing Leven to its present shape and size, about three-and-a-half miles across, covering an area of 4,300 acres.

When I first fished Loch Leven in the early 1950s, Castle Island was a favourite lunch venue. An old, broken, wooded jetty poked into the loch from the south shore and we would moor the boat there and hack our way through the undergrowth to the grey, silent ruins. Since these days, the island has been tidied up; paths constructed, undergrowth cleared, notices planted, explanatory texts displayed. A pleasure boat plies regularly between Kinross and Castle Islands, bringing thousands of visitors each year to the ruined castle. This is called progress. Me, I call it utter nonsense. Little short of historical vandalism. By all means, preserve our ancient monuments; but don't turn them into plastic tourist traps.

There has been a castle on the island, once joined to the mainland by a causeway, since the early fourteenth century and the fortress was one of the key Scottish defensive towers. Shortly after its construction, Lochleven Castle was fully tested. Edward III, breaking the Treaty of Northampton and encouraging the claims of Edward Balliol to the throne of Scotland, did his utmost to sow seeds of rebellion and discontent north of the border.

After the defeat of the Scots at the Battle of Haildon Hill on 19 July, 1333, Balliol was crowned at Scone and by May 1334, King David II and Queen Margaret had fled to France. During the struggles, Lochleven Castle was besieged by the English, who tried, unsuccessfully, to flood out the defenders by blocking the River Leven, thereby raising the level of the loch.

King David's successor, Robert II, grandson of the great King Robert the Bruce and founder of the House of Stewart, was imprisoned in Lochleven Castle in 1368, three years before his accession to the throne of Scotland on 26 March, 1371.

King James I also found Lochleven Castle useful during his unhappy trials and tribulations with the Scottish barons; he had his nephew, Archibald, 5th Earl of Douglas, imprisoned there, suspecting the earl of treacherous, clandestine negotiations with the king's English enemies.

But it was not the English that did for James I, but his own nobles, led by Sir Robert Stewart, the King's grandson and chamberlain, and the Earl of Athol, the king's uncle, along with six others. They murdered their king at the Dominican Abbey of the Blackfriars at Perth, on the night of 21 February 1437. Poor James; eighteen years captive in England, thirteen turbulent years as monarch; ending in squalor, knifed to death in a loathsome sewer.

But the most famous resident of Lochleven Castle was luckless Mary, Queen of Scots, imprisoned there on 16 June, 1567, after the rout of Carberry, when she gave her ungentle husband, Bothwell, permission to flee the field. That he did, rather than stay and face the consequences with his queen, says much about Bothwell's real motives. But in this respect, Bothwell was no different from most of his contemporaries, self-seeking, vain-glorious, pompous, ruthless men, with little time or respect for anything other than their own self-aggrandisement. Bothwell fled to Shetland, and thence to Norway, where he was arrested and sent to Denmark.

The infamous James Hepburn, Earl of Bothwell, hereditary Lord High Admiral of Scotland and husband of Mary, Queen of Scots, eventually died a lunatic in 1578, in Dragsholm prison.

Whilst incarcerated in Lochleven Castle, Mary was forced to abdicate in favour of her infant son, James VI, and, perhaps occasioned by her harsh confinement, Mary lost the twins she was carrying. Nevertheless, by 1 May, 1568, the eve of her dramatic escape from Lochleven, Mary had recovered her spirits, for she wrote to her cousin, Queen Elizabeth I of England, reminding her: "You remember that it has pleased you, divers times, to assure me that if you should see the ring which you sent me, you would help me in all my afflictions . . . For which cause I beg you, seeing these presents, to have pity on your good sister and cousin."

Nineteen years later, on Wednesday, 8 February, 1586, Mary's agony was ended by the headsman's axe; steadfast and courageous to the end, Mary refused the Dean of Peterborough, Dr Fletcher's, entreaties to recant her Catholic faith: "Mr Dean, I am settled in the ancient Catholic Roman religion, and mind to spend my blood in defence of it."

The judicial murder of Mary, Queen of Scots, was a hideous, wicked crime; that her fellow countrymen allowed it to happen is outrageous and unforgivable. James VI may well have been an outstanding monarch, a peerless prince, but to me he is simply the wretch who acquiesced in the torture and imprisonment of his mother; the poor fool who turned a blind eye whilst the English chopped off his mother's head; the man who could hardly wait to abandon Scotland for the tinsel and glitterati of London.

Tinsel and glitterati still abound round Loch Leven, but now in the shape of feathers and fur, dressed on hooks to attract trout, rather than rich apparel to attract human attention and approbation. But here also, ironically, English methods and techniques are affecting traditional Scottish fishing habits.

Because trout now tend to feed on the bottom of the loch, English reservoir lures are increasingly being employed to catch them; weird, hideous creations, more akin to spinning lures than flies: Baby Doll, Ace of Spade, Dog Nobbler, Pearly Nobbler, Pretty Dog and others. These are fished on long leaders, cast miles out from the boat, and then "stripped" back, jerkily, by hand.

Learned papers are written on the best method of retrieving the lure; grown men argue about the relative merits of fast or slow, deep or shallow retrieves, supported by idiotic diagrams purporting to show how the fish reacts to the nobblers, jerking by. The day when I have to resort to raking about the bottom of the loch with lumps of iron is the day I give up fishing. To me this is no more sport than fishing in the Corporation Baths and certainly alien to everything that I hold dear about fishing in Scotland.

Throughout the year, regardless of weather conditions, I stick to the same old, trusted friends: Black Pennel, Ke-He, Soldier Palmer, Loch Ordie, Invicta, March Brown, Greenwell's Glory, Woodcock & Hare-lug, Grouse & Claret, Peter Ross, Alexandria, Silver Butcher, Dunkeld, Silver Invicta. Fished on a short line, on the surface, in front of the boat. If trout will not rise to these flies, fished in that fashion, then they will not rise to anything and are best left in peace to fight another day. If this be error and upon me proved, then no man ever cast, nor ever landed, trout.

Although Loch Leven bestrides the Scottish angling scene like a Colossus, Fife, Kinross and Clackmannan have a host of other excellent trout fisheries where anglers can find good sport: Glenfarg, Glenquoy, Upper and Lower Glendevon, Upper Carriston, Stenhouse, Loch Glow, the Black Loch, Loch Ore Meadows, Carhurlie, Cameron, Lindores, Lochmill and many more. Mostly put and take fisheries, but nonetheless pleasant to fish for that.

Nor are they quite so expensive as Loch Leven seems to have become over the years; and, of course, they are all easily accessible — no Sutherland mountain-goat stuff here — step straight from the car almost into the boat. This makes them very attractive to Lothian anglers, who can finish a hard day's work and then, an hour later, be into their first trout.

All this has been made possible by the building of the Forth Road Bridge. Prior to that, it was quite a different matter and crossing the Forth could take anything up to four hours. There were three ferries, in constant service: one in the middle, the other two loading or unloading at North and South piers. They were called the *William Wallace*, *Robert the Bruce*, and the *Queen Margaret*. Side-paddle steamers.

One of the first times I went across on the ferry was when I was a Boy Scout; I was doing something called, I think, the Adventurer's Badge, for my Queen's Scout certificate, and it was absolutely vital that I got it.

I went down to Queensferry, humped my pack on to the *Queen Margaret* and sailed across the Firth, then set off for Knock Hill and Saline Hill. Camped out on Knock Hill in a raging storm, it was so cold, so wet and windy, that I simply slung the guy ropes between two trees, weighted the skirts down with stones and huddled into my blanket to freeze the night away.

That was my first, cold introduction to the Ochil Hills; but the next morning the sun shone and I walked jauntily down the hill to one of my favourite towns, Scotland's ancient capital city, Dunfermline; where round the top of the Cathedral, written in stone, are the words, "Robert the Bruce".

The great king is buried there. Well, bits of him. When he died, near Dumbarton, he asked his faithful lieutenant, James Douglas, to remove his heart and carry it on the crusade that Bruce had always intended to make to the Holy Land. The heart was duly placed in a silver casket and off Black Douglas went. However, never one to miss a fight, Douglas stopped along the way in Spain, and joined in a battle against the Moors. Rising in his stirrups, Douglas swung the casket round and round his head, then flung it into the thickest of the fight, then spurred his horse in pursuit.

After the battle, Douglas's dead body was found lying over the casket. They left poor Douglas in Spain, but brought the King's heart back to Scotland where it was buried in Melrose Abbey — somewhere. To this day no one knows exactly where.

The casket was made of silver and for many years it has been known that there are seams of silver in the Ochil Hills. In the eighteenth century, Sir John Erskine is reputed to have produced something like £50,000 worth of silver from his mines in the Ochils; and there are also cobalt, copper, lead, and, of course, dusty diamonds: coal.

But for me, that area, and Dunfermline, is inextricably linked with Robert the Bruce, one of my childhood heroes, and I remember recently driving round the Limekilns estate of Lord Elgin, who is descended from the great Scottish King.

Lord Elgin was at the wheel of his white Range Rover and sitting next to him was a Yorkshire agricultural contractor. I was in the back. I was absolutely horrified, when the Yorkshireman, Ray Holt, turned to Lord Elgin and asked, in a conversational sort of way: "Lived round here long then, have you?" Lord Elgin smothered a grunt and replied courteously: "Yes. Actually, about 800 years." I know Yorkshire people, I married a Yorkshire lass, and I cringed, waiting for the inevitable response: "Oh, really? You must almost be one of the locals by now then."

The last chief of Clan Bruce lived at Clackmannan and died there in 1772. But his widow, Mrs Catherine Bruce, survived him long enough to welcome quite a few famous travellers in Scotland; the inevitable Johnson and his sanctimonious lap-dog, Boswell; but perhaps the most famous visitor was Robert Burns, another of my childhood heroes.

Burns was travelling with a Doctor Adair, from Harrogate, and the good doctor made a note of the meeting between Burns and Mrs Catherine Bruce. He reports:

> Visit to Mrs Bruce of Clackmannan. A lady above ninety, the lineal descendant of that race which gave the Scottish throne its highest ornament, interested Burns' feelings. This venerable dame, with characteristic dignity informed me, upon my observing, that I believed that she was descended from the family of Robert Bruce, that Robert Burns was sprung from her family; though deprived of speech by a paralytic affliction, she preserved her hospitality and urbanity. She was in possession of the hero's helmet, and two-handed sword; with which she conferred on Burns, and on myself, the honour of knighthood; remarking that she had a better right to confer that title than some people [King George]. You will of course conclude that the old lady's political tenets were as Jacobite as the poet's.

Another famous family of that era were the Erskines, the Earls of Mar, the most infamous being the earl in charge of the Jacobite forces during the 1715 rebellion; when through masterly inactivity, he failed to win the Battle of Sheriffmuir — although he did not lose it — but certainly lost the Jacobite cause by sitting on his butt doing nothing although he outnumbered Argyll and the government forces three to one.

147

Mar's sister-in-law was Lady Grange, a government supporter, and she is unique in Scottish history as being the only person to have died and been buried three times. She had vastly different political sympathies from her husband and, having overheard some of their plans during a meeting at the Mar house in Edinburgh, confronted her husband and threatened to reveal all to the authorities.

In order to shut her up, Mar had her kidnapped and incarcerated on the Island of Hirta, the largest of the St Kilda isles, sixty miles west of the Outer Hebrides. Lady Grange has the distinction of, as an outsider, having lived on the island, albeit against her will, for longer than anyone else, from 1734 until 1742.

Eventually, in 1742, she was removed to the mainland, where she spent some time in Assynt and then on Skye, where she was taught to spin. She eventually managed to smuggle out a letter which, miraculously, was received by one of her relations in London, telling of her plight. But by the time very much was done about it, the poor soul was really dead.

To cover her kidnap, the plotters had to make it look authentic, so they organised a mock funeral, complete with stone-filled coffin, at Greyfriars Churchyard, Edinburgh; then, when the pursuit was up, and the government sent a warship to find her, another funeral was arranged, this time on the island of Skye, again with a stone-filled coffin. When the poor demented soul eventually did die, she was finally buried at Tumpain Head.

I suppose it comes to us all, that day when we shuffle off to the great trout loch in the sky. When my father's time was approaching, I took him fishing in Fife, one last time. To Loch Fitty, near Dunfermline. Easily accessible, where I could get him afloat with the minimum of discomfort. Caught a few fish, too. A traditional Black Pennel did the damage. Size 14. Dad enjoyed it.

ERICHT AND DUNKELD

ANY of our major roads across the Highlands follow the line of old military roads, built to the order of the Hanoverians after the 1715 rebellion; and perhaps one of the most famous is the A9 from Perth to Inverness.

There is a junction at Dalwhinnie, just north of the high point at Drumochter, where the right fork is still the A9 to Inverness, but the left-hand track used to take soldiers and travellers over the Corrieyairack Pass to the north-west, down to Fort Augustus at the south end of Loch Ness. A busy, important thoroughfare during the eighteenth century; now just a footpath.

Still quite a well-worn footpath and still much travelled, but in the days when it was first built, it would be packed with soldiers and travellers — probably all cursing the intransigent Highlanders responsible for them being there; the wild, kilted men who had dragged them into this God-forsaken land.

The road is an astonishing piece of engineering, given when it was built and the terrain it crosses; twenty-five miles through some of the roughest country in Britain. The pass starts at Fort Augustus, or ends there, depending upon which way you are going, curving up Glen Tarff, which is beautifully wooded on either side. If you have time and energy, I recommend a short fishing diversion; scamper off to the east of the track and explore the series of lochs lying hidden in the hills. They hold some fine sporting trout.

The top of the pass is 896 metres high, and in the days when Corrieyairack was a major military supply route, they used to take carriages over. In 1799 a much travelled lady, Sarah Murray, started to write a series of excellent books describing her journeys in Scotland — the first of an unending flood of Scottish travel books — and one of the redoubtable Sarah's journeys included a description of a passage from Fort Augustus to Dalwhinnie, over Corrieyairack, in a horse and trap.

To get up the steep brae from Fort Augustus to the top of the pass, they needed two plough horses to help; and Sarah recounts the story of a commander, dressing the pass "overall" with his troops and then admiring his colourful handiwork as he surveyed his soldiers, like a red and silver line, snaking up Corrieyairack.

The pass could be a wild place during winter months and several people are known to have died from exposure along the way. Often, to fortify themselves against the journey, travellers would drink too much at Fort Augustus or Dalwhinnie, before setting out, and pay the price of overindulgence with their lives.

Once, a woman and her child, going over the pass with a party of soldiers in winter, refused to move an inch further until she had rested. She was found the following morning, covered in snow, frozen to death. The child survived, blanketed by snow, but warmed by its mother's dying body.

Another famous traveller who used the pass was Bonnie Prince Charlie, when fleeing from the disaster of Culloden in 1746. The Duke of Cumberland, Butcher Cumberland, had established headquarters at Fort Augustus but B.P.C. managed to escape south over the pass, and eventually hid in a secret cave, high above Loch Ericht on the slopes of Ben Alder, known as Cluny's Cave. As you speed up the A9 you catch a fleeting glimpse of the loch, but few people realise that it is one of the longest lochs in Scotland, extending for a distance of nearly seventeen miles, south-west, almost as far as Loch Rannoch.

Ericht is a deep, windy water, full of small, Highland wild brown trout; but there are also some huge monsters in the depths, and fish of over 10lb have been landed, mostly by anglers using the old Scottish fishing method of trolling. Indeed, I am sure that the next British Record Brown Trout could be down there, waiting, mouth agape, ready and anxious to fill your glass case.

The finest description of fishing Loch Ericht and the

neighbouring little River Truim, was written by John Inglis Hall in 1960. Inglis Hall fell in love with Ericht and the Truim and spent many years fishing them from the Dalwhinnie Hotel, in the days when Mr D. C. Matheson was proprietor.

Donald Grant used to gillie and Hall described their first time out together: "Donald in a boat is not exactly a communicative person . . . I do not suppose we spoke a hundred words between the dam at Dalwhinnie and Benalder Cottage, twelve miles down the loch, and not more than five hundred the whole day." Davy Matheson used to say: "Donald's a good man and a great man on the loch, and it keeps him off the drink."

But Donald was ill on the "Day of the Great Fish", and Sandy Craib, another Ericht gillie, witnessed the event which is still talked about at Dalwhinnie.

The day was wild, wet and windy, and the pair trolled a few hundred yards out from the east shore, halfway down the loch. The first fish was a trout of some 2lb 8oz and when Davy landed it he turned to Hall and remarked: "Your net's no' very large. I don't know what we'll do when we get the big one." Their next fish weighed 4lb 8oz. "Never two without three," said Davy, "they're on the take; we might do it."

The third fish hooked was a monster, estimated as being about 12lb in weight, and some eighteen inches too long for the net. They played the great fish for more than half-an-hour, hardly aware of the driving rain and rising gale. Eventually, after several abortive attempts to land the trout, the cast snapped and Davy and Hall watched helplessly as their prize escaped, back to the depths.

Few people fish Ericht, and those who do concentrate their efforts at the south end, in the vicinity of McCook's Bay and where the loch exits via the River Ericht into the cold waters of Loch Rannoch.

McCook's Bay is named after an estate worker who lived there and brought up his family amidst these desolate moorlands and mountains. The story is told that Mr McCook supplemented his income by taking visitors to the site of Bonnie Prince Charlie's cave, which was on the hill above his cottage. But as McCook grew older and less able to make the climb, it is said that he created a new cave, closer and more conveniently located to his cottage. Thus, in his declining years, he could still reap the reward of showing visitors the famous spot where B.P.C. hid.

Loch Ericht is surrounded by intimidating country and a host of Munros, Scotland's mighty 3,000-foot mountains; Carn Dearg, Sgor Gaibhre, Ben Alder, Beinn a' Chlachair, Creag Pitridh, Geal Charn to the north; Carn na Caim, A'buidheanach Bheag, Geal-Charn, A'mharconaich, Beinn Udlamain, Sgairneach Mhor to the south.

The Dalwhinnie Munros are very popular because they are close to the A9 and access is quick and easy; as you step from your car, before you climb an inch, you are already above 1,500 feet, which helps mightily along the way.

Ease of access can, and does, cause conflict between estate owners and lovers of wild places. Scottish estates rely on revenue from sporting lets — shooting, fishing and stalking — and if you have paid dearly for the privileges of shooting a stag, then you are not going to be too amused, after stalking the beast for perhaps three hours over rugged terrain, to have the stag scared off by a group of happy, yellow- and red-clad hikers. No easy matter to resolve, but estates are becoming increasingly aware of the needs and legitimate aspirations of hill walkers and climbers; and few estates manage matters better than Ben Alder, by the shores of Loch Ericht. The head keeper, George Oswald, goes to considerable lengths — and distances — to explain his point of view to hill walkers.

I met George, not at Loch Ericht, but in the centre of Glasgow. It was a bit intimidating, because the venue was the Headquarters of Strathclyde Police, just off Sauchiehall Street. A vast multistorey building. George had travelled down to give a lecture and slide show to the members of the Moray Club, a well-known West of Scotland climbing club. My cousin, Bruce Reynolds, is a member and he had invited me along.

We received a very interesting talk from George, about his life and work as an estate manager and stalker; and he made the point that he was always anxious to welcome hill walkers and climbers on to the estate, but that they should speak to him first, before setting out, so that he could direct them in such a fashion that they would not spoil others' sport and pleasure. He also warns visitors about any new dangers along the way, hazards they should beware of, such as the wild ponies they use to bring stags off the hill, who seem to live on a diet of car wing-mirrors and aerials.

After the lecture, I was standing blethering to my cousin when we discovered, to our dismay, that everyone had left and we were alone in the lecture hall; having, might I say, climbed about seventy-five Munros in our imagination. We were absolutely lost. We wandered about the building, going up and down in lifts, of which there seemed to be half-a-dozen on each floor, and before long we hadn't a clue where we were, north, south, east or west.

It was very embarrassing, but eventually we stopped shooting up and down lifts, walking endless miles along empty, echoing corridors, and found an office with a telephone. Here we were, hill walkers and compass and map experts, lost in the centre of Glasgow. Couldn't find our way out of the building, let alone up a mountain.

I picked up the phone and dialled the exchange and said "Excuse me . . ." but before I could get another word out a very cross policeman snapped: "That's where you blighters are. Stay there. Don't move a muscle. We will come and get you." Five minutes later we were ushered ignominiously out on to Sauchiehall Street, red-faced and abashed. I have never been so embarrassed in all my life.

The first time I went over the Drumochter Pass to Inverness was to the Royal Highland Show, in 1955, before the Society found a permanent site at Ingliston. It was a remarkable journey, and I particularly remember the River Garry, which runs by the side of the railway line. Then, it was a mighty, tumbling Highland river, pushing its way through rocky gorges, urgent with white foam, banks decked with rowan. Now, the poor river has almost completely disappeared, a raped shadow of its former self; the glory gone, drained to provide power for soap-opera television and ready-to-cook meals. What a sad stream. In summer there is barely a trickle. Hardly enough to wet a decent dram. What kind of twisted logic can claim that such pointless, wanton destruction is progress?

South from Loch Ericht, in the gently wooded hills round Dunkeld, lies another beautiful Scottish loch, Loch of the Lowes, famous for its osprey which have nested there for many years. There are three interconnected waters, linked together by the Lunan Burn, and Lowes is a nature reserve, a delight for waders and ducks: clockwork coot, crow-black, white-nebbed, ticking through the reeds as though wound up; statuesque heron; cautious mallard.

The surrounding woods are alive with finch and tits; I saw my first jay, flashing bright-winged through these forests, and, in the hills above Lowes, my first capercaillie, a huge, ungainly, turkey-like bird, squawking angrily at being disturbed.

The reserve is carefully managed and maintained by the Scottish Wildlife Trust, so if you don't know a lot about birds, and want to learn more, Lowes is the place to go; there is always somebody there to give advice and help, take you to the hides, point out birds of special interest.

Butterstone Loch, near by, is the place for anglers, although it too is a delight for ornithologists; but on Butterstone, there is more looking into the water than peering into the sky.

Craiglush is the third loch and all these waters used to be coarse fisheries. Quite unusual for Scotland, where coarse fish are ruthlessly netted out in order to protect salmon, sea-trout and brown trout stocks.

Coarse fish are present in many Scottish waters, particularly in South-West Scotland, where they are tolerated; but further north, fishery managers fight a constant battle against the unwelcome attentions of pike, the freshwater shark, which can create havoc in a trout fishery. And believe me, Jack pike is a difficult fellow to eliminate. He seems to be able to survive against all odds, and in spite of best efforts, there are still pike in the Dunkeld waters. But they are under control and Butterstone has been stocked with rainbow trout which thrive and grow to considerable size.

Many anglers might turn their noses up at the thought of fishing for hatchery reared rainbow trout in a put-and-take fishery. However, these are fish of very high quality and they give an excellent account of themselves. Butterstone is a welcome venue for people from Perth, Dundee and Edinburgh; and the road system is much improved, bringing Butterstone within one hour's drive from the capital.

We fished Butterstone a couple of years ago, as a family. All the children were taught to fish at an early age and still enjoy the sport; and for me, fishing provides the only opportunity I now have of beating my sons at anything. I gave up long ago on physical sports; and recently, bridge and chess have gone the same way; but fishing is different. I generally manage to hold my own. Makes me feel less old.

That particular expedition was during a day of blazing sun and dead flat calm. We roasted whilst the fish sulked on the bottom; and we did more sunbathing than fishing. We saw the osprey from Loch of the Lowes. He popped over for lunch and did better than most.

We fished all day without catching a single thing, refusing to rake about the bottom with lures and lead-core lines. We all feel the same; if you can't catch fish rising to a fly on the surface, then, in our opinion, you should leave them alone.

In the early evening, a mist came down, shimmering grey over the loch, fingering into the reeds, darkening the trees. We pulled shorewards, and as we did so, I saw my wife, Ann, with daughter-in-law, Barbara, and second son, Charlie, appearing through the mist, like King Arthur's barge, heading towards Avalon. Charles had tied a white handkerchief to the handle of the landing net and was waving it in surrender.

However, when all the anglers gathered outside the excellent boathouse, we discovered quite a few fish had been taken, and very nice they looked too — the fish, not the anglers; the fishermen tended to be of the multi-pocket waistcoat, badge-bedecked brigade; but some had done well. One angler, a local architect, had four magnificent fish.

When the going gets tough on Butterstone, it is always possible to escape to Dunkeld, resting on the banks of the sweetly flowing Tay. Always looking freshly brushed neat and tidy. My wife's ancestors come from Dunkeld, on her mother's side, where the family name is Blair.

Escape is an appropriate term, when applied to Dunkeld, because in 1689, that is what most of the inhabitants of Dunkeld did. A force of government soldiers, 1,200 in number, were given the task of defending Dunkeld from the Highland Host, fresh from their famous victory at the Battle of Killiecrankie "where claymores got a prankie o' ". Although their commander, brilliant Bonnie Dundee had been killed, the Highland army were still in high spirits and determined to wreak havoc on Dunkeld. It was an ill-matched fight, with the government force greatly outnumbered, but it raged all day, with the government troops furiously defending two substantial houses in the middle of town, close to the cathedral.

At nightfall, tired and weary, the Highlanders rested, finding houses round the town where they could sleep. The commander of the government forces had been killed, as had been the second in command, but Captain Munro, the next most senior officer, now devised an audacious plan.

He selected twelve men from his weary troop and sent them on a suicide mission. They crept up on the buildings where the Highlanders were sleeping, barred the doors, and then set them on fire. A lot of kilts were singed that night and the Highlanders fled in disarray.

But of course, it didn't do much for the town. Dunkeld was completely destroyed; and as dawn broke over the smouldering ruins, the only buildings left relatively intact were the two that housed the stout defenders. The rest of the town was in ruins.

That is how Scotland got its first new town. Embryonic town planners set to work and rebuilt Dunkeld; and did a magnificent job, creating the lovely square and the charming buildings clustered near the ancient cathedral.

If you want to get back to nature, you can cross the Tay and the new A9 and visit the Hermitage on the River Braan, two miles west of town, a wonderful walk through magnificent woodlands to the building overlooking the falls. The Hermitage was built in 1758, by the son-in-law of the second Duke of Atholl, and was also known as Ossian's Hall.

I have very fond memories of the Hermitage. Also, actually, of sleeping in the middle of the A9. Or at least, where the A9 now runs. We camped there, many years ago, as Boy Scouts, at Inver Park, and we used to play wide games up the River Braan. Even as a youngster, I still appreciated the beauty of the surroundings, but we were probably more interested in tracking, than matters arboreal.

I remember having a splendid fight round Ossian's Cave, a vaulted, turf and earth-covered building, just above the falls; my patrol, the Otters, were to attack and take the cave which was being guarded by our arch-enemies, the Beavers, led by my friend, William Calder.

I led my patrol up the course of the river, stumbling and splashing through the water, and just before the falls, scaled the steep banks and fell upon the unsuspecting Beavers. Happy memories. So I know the Braan very well. After the fight we swam in the deep, crystal-clear pool below the falls. I can still feel the caress of the soft, cold water on my body. Saw a trout as well.

In retrospect, I think that I was overawed by the magnificence of the trees. I recall, during a night game, being alone on the moonlight, surrounded by their mighty columns, half-afraid, and yet transfixed by their majesty. I had never seen such tall trees. They seemed to go upwards for ever, touching heaven itself. Mythical and fairy-like.

Ossian, a blend of fact and fantasy, is one of the great characters in Scottish mythology. He didn't lose many battles, but there is a story told about one that he did. To cheer him up after this defeat, he was spirited away by the daughter of the King of the Land of Eternal Youth, where he remained for 300 years, before returning to his cave overlooking the falls.

Less mythical is Miss Georgina Ballantine's record-breaking salmon, caught downstream from Dunkeld, at Caputh in October 1922. The fish weighed 64lb and is the largest rod-and-line-caught salmon ever landed in the British Isles. Miss Ballantine was the daughter of a Tay boatman and her magnificent achievement secured her a place in angling's "Land of Eternal Youth".

We poor mortal men have been trying, unsuccessfully, to emulate Miss Ballantine's feat ever since. But it is a well-known fact that any one lady angler is far more efficient than any ten men. Ossian included; so I suspect that we are going to have a very long wait indeed before Miss Ballantine's record tumbles.

AWE

RGYLL and the Western Isles were once almost a separate kingdom, ruled by Clan Donald, the mighty Lords of the Isles. It took successive Scottish kings several centuries to break the power of the Lordship of the Isles and turn them into subservient, respectful subjects. Indeed, there are those who claim that Clan Donald are still a law unto themselves; and having spent many a fine day wandering in their lands, I for one agree.

Argyllshire is raked by long, fjord-like fingers, probing into the heart of Scotland. Running north-east, south-west, all at the same angle. Almost as though some giant, angry hand has clawed its way across the land, gouging out the western seaboard. And one of the longest scars is filled by Loch Awe, which extends for a distance of nearly twenty-six miles. A freshwater loch, full of brown trout, salmon, sea-trout, and increasingly today, escapee rainbow trout from fish farms. Some of these fish now seem to be breeding in Loch Awe, and trout of great size are caught.

Loch Awe is one of the last bastions of the myth of free fishing, a place where anything goes. It is a popular misconception that brown trout fishing in Scotland is free, but this is not the case. Trout are considered in law to be wild animals and as such, they belong to the person who captures them. But the right to capture them belongs to the owner of the land through which the river flows, or borders the loch where the trout lie. To take fish without proper permission is a civil offence and the riparian owner is entitled to use any reasonable force to stop people from infringing his rights.

Sadly, as far as Loch Awe is concerned, things have got to such a state that water bailiffs and owners now find it almost impossible to deal with the increasing number of poachers who descend on the loch from as far afield as the Midlands of England. Nor do these unwelcome visitors fish in a fair and reasonable fashion. More often than not they spin, worm, net and maggot fish. One rod is rarely enough, most have half-a-dozen propped up on stones along the bank, and success is measured only in terms of numbers of fish killed.

Recently, 500,000 rainbow trout escaped from a fish farm near the Pass of Brander at the north end of Loch Awe and by the following weekend 700 so-called anglers were lining the banks hauling them in by their thousands; and leaving behind shores littered with tons of rubbish and refuse.

In 1985 the Loch Awe Improvement Association L.A.I.A. was formed by a number of riparian owners "in an effort to prevent abuse of the loch and lochside", but the L.A.I.A. claim that their attempt to obtain voluntary co-operation was ignored. Therefore, in order to protect their interests the L.A.I.A. applied to the Secretary of State for Scotland for a Protection Order, under the terms of the Freshwater Fishery (Scotland) Act, 1976.

Astonishingly, more than 100 objections were lodged and the Awe & Avoch Amenity Association A.A.A.A. was formed with the sole objective of fighting the proposal for a Protection Order. The A.A.A.A. claim that the L.A.I.A. is not fully representative of all Loch Awe riparian owners and that it was established more to protect fish-farming interests than to protect the Aweside environment and the brown trout for which the loch is famous.

In one sense, the A.A.A.A. is absolutely right. The escape of so many rainbow trout into Loch Awe is nothing less than a major ecological disaster, not only for the loch, but for the adjacent feeder streams and rivers, such as the Orchy. Stocks of indigenous brown trout, salmon parr and sea-trout will be decimated by rapacious rainbow trout and indeed the foreign invaders could, in time, completely wipe out native stock. But it is wrong to suggest that fishing pressure on Loch Awe has increased to intolerable levels only because of fish-farming and escapee rainbow trout; and that until the advent of fish-farming, everything in Loch Awe was lovely; that visiting anglers were paragons of virtue and always well behaved.

As is so often the case, the facts are somewhat different. I have been fishing Loch Awe since the late 1960s and even then it was obvious that the "free-fishing" mentality encouraged massive abuse. I have seen anglers taking boxes of trout home with them, determined to make a profit by selling them to hotels in Glasgow and the south. And the intervening years have brought thousands more people into angling, in both England and Scotland, all brought up on the daft doctrine of scientific fishing assiduously peddled by most angling magazines and tackle manufacturers. The concept of fair play and sportsmanship does not sell rods and reels; consequently, such "archaic" nonsense is rarely given house-room by editors.

Because of its beauty and accessibility, many anglers arrive at Loch Awe, light of battle glinting in their eyes, determined at all costs not to leave until they have packed their freezers to the gunnel; and the sad result is the present conflict. Alarmed landowners trying to protect their property: angling clubs, fearful that their activities will be curtailed and subjected to bureaucratic controls.

In the meantime, it is business as usual for the ugly, free-for-all brigade and until riparian owners and other loch-users get their act together and agree a policy for the protection of this priceless asset, Loch Awe will continue to be destroyed. Which is sad, and very bad news for future generations of Scottish anglers.

Loch Awe had, and still has, an enviable reputation in Scotland for producing very large trout. The unofficial, all-time British Record Brown Trout is reputed to have come from Loch Awe; the fish was caught in 1866 and was said to have weighed 39lb 8oz. Even in more recent years, trout and ferox of great size are regularly taken from Loch Awe and fish of up to nearly 20lb are sometimes caught.

There is a special, old, much tried Scottish technique for catching these monsters, called trolling. You use a bare hook, and on it you tie a trout of about 10oz. This is attached to a lead-core line, to make it sink, and the lure is trailed behind a slowly moving boat, at a depth of some twenty to thirty feet. The lure, that is, not the boat. Fingers crossed, up and down the loch, waiting for some monster to bite.

Some anglers become so engrossed with the capture of ferox that they fish for nothing else; scouring the deep, cold lochs of Scotland for that elusive "one for the glass case"; and they have plenty of waters to choose from, for Scotland abounds with excellent ferox lochs: Sionascaig, Assynt, Veyatie, Arkaig, Garry, Quoich, Inchlaggan, Morar, Rannoch, Laidon, and many more.

A few years ago, I was invited to join a team of anglers, sponsored by that great Scots fisherman, Hector Maclennan, of Ballantines Whisky, attempting to break the Scottish Brown Trout Record. The venue was Glen Garry and Loch Quoich, where all the previous record fish had been caught.

The attack was to be mounted in shifts, three every twenty-four hours, for six days, two anglers fishing all the time, night and day. Never having trolled before, and not relishing such an assault course, I declined the offer; and although a number of fish of over 15lb were in fact caught, the record remained intact, just under 20lb.

Loch Awe is very beautiful, particularly in the spring, graced by wonderful woodlands, sunlight slanting through branches, dappling the water; daffodils nodding, the surface of the loch shining, a superb picture of all that is best about Scotland's countryside. A magic place; and even more so when trout are rising.

One spring, whilst staying at Ford, I got talking to a man who turned out to be a minor TV personality. Lew Gardiner, an interviewer. Lew had never fly-fished before and so I agreed to introduce him to the gentle art. The following day we met near Portsonachan and began our lesson.

Lew was one of my more difficult pupils and I have had a few over the years. The problem was that he would hardly stop talking long enough for me to give any meaningful instruction. The moment I paused, whilst rehearsing basic facts, such as tucking the elbow in, Lew would be off on some adventure; recounting what he had said to Moshe Dyan, or what General Gowan had said to him. Eventually, I gave up. Retreating to a soft, primrose be-decked bank, I left Lew to get on with it and soon fell asleep in the warm April sunlight. I was rudely awakened by being slapped on the face by the tails of half-a-dozen very nice trout. "Thank's, Bruce, that was great fun. Come, the bar's open."

We were halfway down our first pint when Lew spotted Humphrey Atkins, then, if I remember correctly, Northern Ireland Secretary. I felt sorry for Mr Atkins, obviously enjoying, or hoping to enjoy, a few days' peace and quiet. Lew descended like a wolf on the fold. I finished my pint and went back to the loch.

The woodlands surrounding Loch Awe look very natural, but they are in fact the result of man's endeavours over the centuries; managed for hundreds of years, to supply the timber used in producing charcoal for iron smelting, during the seventeenth and eighteenth centuries. Woods were copiced, the ancient art of woodland management, which now, sadly, seems to have given way to boom or burst, mono-culture, blanket, conifer afforestation. What they did was to fell the tree, making sure that a goodly stump was left, which fooled the roots into believing that they still had a job to do. New branches sprouted, and every thirty or forty years, these shoots were cropped. Thus maintaining a regular supply of timber.

If you follow the very twisting lochside road north, you eventually arrive at Bonawe, on Loch Etive, and there, marvellously preserved, are the old iron works on the shores of the loch. The iron ore came in by sea and there is an excellent industrial museum at the foundry site at Bonawe Furnace.

Timber was used for iron smelting throughout Scotland, although, sadly, the forests were not all as well managed as Loch Awe woodlands; there is a place called Furnace on the north shore of Loch Maree in Wester Ross, whilst just to the south of Loch Awe, there is another Furnace; so it shows the importance of iron smelting to the Scottish economy at that time, the Second Scottish Iron Age.

The original trees were once part of the ancient oak woods that covered vast areas of central Scotland, but if you go back through the Pass of Brander, you come to an altogether more modern industrial power development. The great hydroelectric scheme carved into the very heart of Ben Cruachan, where the River Awe hurries northwards to meet Loch Etive.

The Awe has always been noted for the size of its salmon and fish of over 50lb have been caught in days past. Now, sadly, with the impounding of the waters in the hydroelectric scheme, the old days have vanished and runs of salmon have drastically declined, both in the River Awe, and its principal tributary, the River Orchy.

Cruachan was the Campbell war-cry, which they screamed as they rushed into battle, roaring the name of their great mountain in defiance: "Cruachan, Cruachan". In our family, we refer to the peak as Mount Kraken; not as a mark of disrespect, but because that is how Lew Gardiner once pronounced it, when I suggested that we indulge in some hill-loch fishing: "If you think you are getting me anywhere near Mount Kraken, you are off your tiny head, Bruce," he exploded. Mount Kraken it has remained, ever since.

Clan Campbell had the knack of backing the winner in the turbulent times of Scotland's formative years; there were plenty of disputes to give them a lot of practice and they always seemed to come out on top. They prospered mightily as a race and always played an important part in Scottish affairs; but the old saying, "it is a far cry from Loch Awe" had a double meaning, depending upon when and by whom it was used.

If the Campbells themselves used the phrase, it meant that no matter where they were in the world, if they were in difficulty or in trouble, some member of the clan was bound to be near by, ready to come to their aid. If the phrase was used by their enemies, it meant: "Look here Campbell, you are on your own this time and need not look for help from the rest of your damned clan."

One place where help is definitely required is whilst afloat on Loch Awe. At times the loch can be very wild and windy and to venture out in a boat anything less than absolutely seaworthy is to court disaster; the many tragic accidents that have happened over the years attest to this fact.

The Vikings used Loch Awe as a "road" and had a much better idea of what size of boat was appropriate for this vast, dangerous water. They transported longships overland and sailed the loch, spreading their reign of terror far into the heart of Scotland.

Viking crews invented the trade union movement. They had a strict set of rules governing employment, and of how the business of rape, rob and pillage should be conducted. For instance, the cook, as far as possible, had to be put ashore at least once a day, to prepare a hot meal. Another condition concerned the division of booty: everyone had an equal share, and the captain got in addition what was called the boat's share. Very much as is still done today in modern fishing boats. The third rule was that if you had to bail the boat more than three times during the course of any one day, then the contract was null and void. Everybody could abandon ship with impunity and go home. Which I must confess reminds me of many of the vessels that Ann and I have had to contend with on Scottish lochs. Your average Viking wouldn't have set foot in them. Nor would they have relished some of the packed lunches we have had to cope with. The worst was the cold curry sandwiches. Greasy and dripping. Left-overs from the previous night's dinner.

It was a very cold day, in April, and we were drifting near the islands off the north shore. The prospect of lunch was the only thing keeping us going and when, after the first bite, we realized the full horror of the situation, we quickly abandoned ship and headed for the nearest shop.

That evening, our host inquired politely if we had enjoyed lunch. We grunted, rather than have a row on our first day; but the next morning, before setting off, we checked the lunch box. Sure enough, Cold lamb. Last night's main course.

We established a pattern. Once out of sight of the hotel, lunch was quickly dumped and we descended on the village shop to stock up. However, I'm sure that our perfidious actions were reported back to the hotel, because each evening, with painful courtesy, we would be asked: "Did you enjoy your lunch, gentlemen?"

We once visited Loch Awe as a family, staying at Ford with friends, Tony Sykes and his wife and family from Glasgow. One morning we arrived at the mooring bay, the lagoon at the south end called the Loden; there is an old, rotting jetty, a relic of the days when steamers used to ply the loch.

We parked our cars and Tony, much to my surprise, gave in to the pleading of the children and agreed to take them for a trip round the bay, prior to us setting out to fish. All six children clambered into the boat and off Sykes went, grinning from ear to ear.

We sat in the car whilst Sykes played happy families, and eventually he returned to the jetty. Now Sykes casts a large shadow, and as he approached, he stood up to stop the outboard motor. As he turned round, his ample behind nudged his trout-rod, which he had taken, just in case a fish rose, and we watched in horror as the rod slipped out of the boat, almost in slow motion, and disappeared from sight.

This was not just an ordinary rod, but one that had belonged to his grandfather; a dream of a rod, a Hardy Perfection. We looked at each other and wondered what on earth we were going to say to him and who was to break the news. Well, I always seem to get landed with these tasks, so I explained to Sykes, as gently as I could, exactly what had happened. He thought I was joking and went back to the boat to check, even searching under the seats in mounting despair.

But Tony has always been a lucky sort of a man. A couple of weeks later, in a Glasgow bar, he overheard two men talking about an expedition their club had planned to Loch Awe. The club concerned was a diving club. It took Sykes about half a second to explain his problem, and strike a bargain. Ten days later, he reported the recovery of his rod. Arc lights had to be used and it took hours of careful searching, but the rod was found — in perfect condition — with a six-pound trout firmly attached to one of the flies.

But I didn't buy that one.

SELECT BIOGRAPHY

Bennet, Donald, *The Munros* (Scottish Mountaineering Trust, Edinburgh)

Bennet, Donald, *The Scottish Highlands* (Scottish Mountaineering Trust, Edinburgh)

Bingham, Caroline, *Land of the Scots* (Fontana, London)

Burnett, Ray, *Benbecula* (Mingulay Press, Benbecula)

Butterfield, Irvine, *The High Mountains of Britain and Ireland* (Diadem Books, London)

Dickie, John M. (Ed) *Great Angling Stories* (Chambers, Edinburgh)

Dunkeld and Birnam (Perth, Dunkeld and Birnam Tourist Association)

Feacham, Richard, *Guide to Prehistoric Scotland* (Batsford Press, London)

Gordon, Seaton, *Highways and Byways in the West Highlands* (Macmillan, London)

Grimble, Ian, *The Trial of Patrick Sellar* (Routledge & Kegan Paul, London)

Fergusson, W. *Scotland, 1689 to the Present* (Mercat Press, Edinburgh)

Hall, John Inglis, *Fishing a Highland Stream* (Putnam & Co, London)

Hendry, George, *Midges in Scotland* (Aberdeen University Press, Aberdeen)

Hogg, James, *Highland Tours* (Byway Books, Hawick)

Johnson, Stephen, *Fishing from Afar* (Peter Davies, London)

Lindsay, Maurice, *The Lowlands of Scotland* (Robert Hale, London)

166

MacKenzie, Agnes Mure, *Scottish Pageant* (Oliver & Boyd, Edinburgh)

MacKenzie, Alexander, *History of the Highland Clearances* (Melven Press, Inverness)

Massie, Allan, *101 Great Scots* (Chambers, Edinburgh)

Melrose Abbey (HMSO, Edinburgh)

Murray, W. H., *The Companion Guide to the West Highlands of Scotland* (Collins, London)

Nicholson, R., *Scotland, The Later Middle Ages* (Mercat Press, Edinburgh)

Omand, Donald, *The Caithness Book* (Highland Printers, Inverness)

Poucher, W. A., *The Scottish Peaks* (Constable, London)

Prebble, John, *Highland Clearances* (Penguin, Harmondsworth)

Prebble, John, *Culloden* (Secker & Warburg, London)

Roberts, John, *The New Illustrated Dictionary of Trout Flies* (George Allen & Unwin, London)

Robson, Michael J. H., *Tibbie Shiels* (Ovenshank, Newcastleton)

Sandison, Bruce, *Hill Walkers Guide to Scotland* (Unwin Hyman, London)

Sandison, Bruce, *Sporting Gentleman's Gentleman* (Unwin Hyman, London)

Sandison, Bruce, *Trout Lochs of Scotland* (Unwin Hyman, London)

Scottish National Portrait Gallery, *Scott and his Circle* (National Galleries of Scotland, Edinburgh)

Steel, Tom, *The Life and Death of St Kilda* (Fontana, London)

Thompson, Francis, *Northern Scotland and the Islands* (Michael Joseph, London)

Thorne and Collocett (Ed), *Chambers Biographical Dictionary* (Chambers, Edinburgh)